A Year of Russian Feasts

CATHERINE CHEREMETEFF JONES

Illustrations by Barbara Stott McCoy

BANTAM BOOKS

LONDON • NEW YORK • TORONTO • SYDNEY • AUCKLAND

A YEAR OF RUSSIAN FEASTS
A BANTAM BOOK: 0 553 81613 6

Originally published in the United States by Jellyroll Press
First publication in Great Britain

PRINTING HISTORY
Bantam edition published 2003

1 3 5 7 9 10 8 6 4 2

Copyright © Catherine C. G. Jones 2002

The right of Catherine Cheremeteff Jones to be identified as
the author of this work has been asserted in accordance with
sections 77 and 78 of the Copyright Designs and Patents Act 1988.

Every effort has been made to obtain the necessary permissions with reference
to copyright material, both illustrative and quoted; should there be any omissions
in this respect we apologize and shall be pleased to make the appropriate
acknowledgements in any future edition.

Set in 11/16pt Garamond by
Falcon Oast Graphic Art Ltd.

Bantam Books are published by Transworld Publishers,
61–63 Uxbridge Road, London W5 5SA,
a division of The Random House Group Ltd,
in Australia by Random House Australia (Pty) Ltd,
20 Alfred Street, Milsons Point, Sydney, NSW 2061, Australia,
in New Zealand by Random House New Zealand Ltd,
18 Poland Road, Glenfield, Auckland 10, New Zealand
and in South Africa by Random House (Pty) Ltd,
Endulini, 5a Jubilee Road, Parktown 2193, South Africa.

Printed and bound in Great Britain by
Cox & Wyman Ltd, Reading, Berkshire.

Papers used by Transworld Publishers are natural, recyclable
products made from wood grown in sustainable forests. The
manufacturing processes conform to the environmental
regulations of the country of origin.

FOR MY GRANDMOTHER

AND MOTHER

Acknowledgments

My greatest debt of gratitude goes to all of my Russian friends who shared their homes, meals, recipes, and hearts with me. Their names fill the pages of this book and without them there simply would be no book. Anna Kourakova, Antonina Malinina, Lena Mesnikova, Natalya Ryadnova, and her son, Pavel (Paul) Lebedev, embraced me like family. I thank them all for their love and friendship over the years.

Closer to home, I am grateful to my mother, Marie Abernethy, and my grandmother, Katherine Cheremeteff, for teaching me the pleasures of the table and the kitchen. It is a special gift to have grown up in a kitchen of loving cooks. The generosity and encouragement of my stepfather, Bob Abernethy, are as fresh today as when I started this project in Moscow. I would also like to thank my father, Brandon Grove, Jr., his wife Mariana, my mother-in-law, Evelyn Jones, Paul and Martha Grove, and my brother Mark for their tremendous support.

I thank Susan Derecskey for her thoughtful and graceful style of editing. Judith Sutton's copy-editing skills are exceptional, but even more, I value our friendship which dates back to cooking school days in Paris. Barbara Stott McCoy's gentle and intuitive nature are reflected in her exquisite illustrations. The interior layout is the work of Deborah Rust, a perfectionist with an unparalleled eye for beauty.

I thank Kathleen Luft for her unwavering enthusiasm and Russian language editing. I am indebted to James O'Shea Wade for coming up with the title one snowy afternoon in New York, and to Lisa Natanson for all of her editorial suggestions. I am grateful to Elizabeth Langworthy for her advice, and to many other friends who have helped along the way including, Ellen Moulier, Sandra Vonetes, C. Leigh Gerber, Father Constantine White, and Patrick Wingate. A special thanks to Martha Casselman and Lisa Ekus for their encouragement over the years, and to Francesca Liversidge and her team at Transworld Publishers for discovering my book and sharing it abroad.

My family, Paul, Aleksandra and Hale, are my constant sources of strength, inner peace, and joy. There are no words to thank them enough.

Contents

Love without slinking doubt
and love your best,
And threaten, if you threaten,
not in jest,
And if you lose your temper,

Lose it all, and let your blow straight
from the shoulder fall;
In altercation, boldly speak
your view,
And punish but when
punishment is due;
With both hands forgiveness give away;
And if you feast,
Feast till the break of day.

—Aleksey Konstantinovich Tolstoy

Introduction

OREIGNERS WHO SPEND TIME IN RUSSIA soon learn that there are actually two Russias – one public and the other private. The public Russia is typically cold and dark, backward and wary. The private Russia – the Russia of tea at a friend's kitchen table or of sautéed mushrooms in a village *dacha* – is almost unfailingly cozy and kind. It is this Russia that I discovered through my Russian friends, who invited me into their homes and took me into their confidence.

From 1991 to 1994, I lived in Moscow with my mother, Marie Cheremeteff Abernethy, a descendant of the Sheremetev clan of the Romanov dynasty, and my stepfather, Bob Abernethy, who was on a five-year assignment for NBC News. Those three years were some of the most exciting and turbulent times in recent Russian history. Communism was on the verge of collapse and Yeltsin was trying desperately to convince his fellow citizens that democracy was the path of the future. Gorbachev's ideas of *glasnost* and *perestroika*, loosely defined as 'openness' and 'restructuring,' did in fact create a more accessible Russia, one that allowed me to make Russian friends, enter Russian homes, and explore Russian traditions and culture—all things that would have been difficult, if not impossible, under Communism.

As I pursued my culinary journey, I began to unravel the strings that connect Russian cuisine to country life, history, the Orthodox Church, and the changing seasons. The deepest roots of contemporary Russian cuisine lie in the foodways of village life, which have always followed the rhythm of the seasons. Spring is the time for planting; summer for preserving fruits and salting and pickling vegetables; autumn for gathering and drying mushrooms; and winter for relaxing around the fire with simple food and good company.

Whether in a village home or a city apartment, Russian kitchens showcase the same dishes, although somewhat refined, as they did centuries ago. Soups and stews simmer for hours in onion-shaped pots called *chaguns*, sweet and savory pies are baked for special occasions, and an endless array of potato, beet, and cabbage dishes tells the story of a people who live at a latitude of long winters and short growing seasons.

Atop these centuries-old traditions, Russia's nineteenth-century aristocrats layered a sophisticated, French-influenced cuisine that lasted as long as they did. In contrast to the simple yet tasty everyday meals of the common people, the uninhibited opulence of the Russian aristocracy had no limits. Following Catherine the Great's lead, every noble family who could afford one had a French chef. Food costs at imperial balls were of no concern, family fortunes would be squandered on a single feast, and tables literally buckled from the weight of their splendor. 'A single goose was too much for one person and not enough for two,' an old saying went.

This short-lived era of imported fancy foods and exotic hothouse produce left almost no lasting mark on contemporary Russian fare, except perhaps outside Russia's borders. During three years of dining in Russian homes, I was never served a Charlotte Russe, Strawberries Romanov, Beef Stroganov, Chicken Kiev, or any of the other typically European-influenced Russian dishes that seem to be more popular on Western menus than on Russian ones. What I did eat in Russian homes was delicious food lovingly prepared by skillful cooks.

Communism wiped out the Russian aristocracy and its opulence. Communist ideology denigrated all taste and style and promoted the industrial canned goods highlighted in Soviet-era cookbooks. The scarcity of fresh ingredients in stores and markets made preparing good meals a challenge. Dingy restaurants in Intourist hotels reserved for foreigners produced a ghastly assortment of barely edible dishes from processed meats and canned vegetables, notably anemic peas and carrots. Desserts were nondescript and the service was notoriously rude and inefficient. Most visitors to the Soviet Union left with a deservedly bad impression of Russian food.

But despite the extravagance of the nobles and the hardships of Communism, good Russian home cooking survived. Two bedrocks of Russian life keep its cuisine alive—the *dacha* and the Russian Orthodox Church. The word *dacha* refers to a plot of land in the countryside, with or without a house on it. The more symbolic definition is a place of retreat where Russians go to re-energize their bodies and souls by being part of nature's growing cycle. Tending their gardens, eating the fruits of their labor, and storing some for later are traditions that sustain the Russian table.

Feast days of the Russian Orthodox Church have kept Russia's finest and richest celebratory dishes intact despite history, despite hardship, despite everything. Easter's *bliny* (Butter Week pancakes), *kulich* (Easter bread), and *paskha* (Easter cheesecake) are religiously prepared in homes every year, as they have been for centuries. And the Russian Orthodox Church continues to determine menus in many homes—during the one hundred or so fast days and the numerous feast days of the liturgical year.

The forty recipes in this book are the best from my Russian collection. I can say without reservation that these dishes taste as good away from Russian soil as they do in the coziness of a *dacha* or beside a soul-warming samovar. They come from the yellowing pages of notebooks of my Russian friends, from cooks whose memory is their only guide, and from my mother's and grandmother's kitchens, where recipes call for a pinch of this and a handful of that. There is a good story behind every one of them.

My mentors in the Russian kitchen were Natalya and Antonina. Natalya, a retired journalist who devoted her time to her choir group and her grandchildren, taught me the joys of the Russian Easter table as well as everyday meals. Antonina, a retired nurse who filled her days with cooking for family and friends, shared with me the art of making fruit preserves and introduced me to the spiritual ritual of tea. A native of Siberia, she also taught me how to make real Siberian *pelmeny* (meat-filled dumplings) and how to eat them.

Anna included me in her family's festive New Year's Eve celebrations and invited me to a Russian civil wedding ceremony. Galina, a cook at Danilovsky Monastery, gave me a behind-the-scenes tour of Easter traditions in the monastery kitchen—I was the first American ever to be invited backstage. Viktor, a fun-loving retired baker, included me in his family's birthday celebrations. Lena chose me to be her daughter's godmother, and Mark and Masha prepared memorable vegetarian dinners in their communal apartment.

Natalya's husband, Yevgeny, invited me to his childhood home in the village of Kosilova, where I experienced the mystical ritual of mushroom hunting. He introduced me to his lifelong neighbor, Mariya, who lived off her land as her family had done for centuries. Mariya welcomed me into her home and showed me firsthand how a Russian villager provides for the winter.

It was through these people and experiences that I discovered the timeless world of Russian cuisine, customs, and traditions. My Russian friends introduced me to the real Russia, the private Russia, the Russia that enters the heart and warms the soul.

Vegetarian Dinner
in a Communal Apartment

As soon as he noticed that a guest had only one piece left on his plate he helped himself to another, saying as he did so, 'Without a mate neither man nor bird can live in the world.' If the visitor had two pieces on his plate, he helped himself to a third, saying, 'Two isn't much of a number is it? God loves trinity.' If the guest ate all three, he would say, 'Have you ever seen a cart with only three wheels? And who builds a cottage with only three corners?' For four he had another saying, and for five, too.

—Nikolay Gogol, *Dead Souls*

*A*S ALL VISITORS TO RUSSIA LEARN, usually to their delight, sometimes to their distress, the Russians are people of extraordinary extremes. A cold, expressionless exterior can mask a warm, generous heart, and the sacrificial hospitality of the poor, even in hard times, is legendary. Within the few crowded rooms of a Russian apartment, away from the ugliness and cold of the street, a Russian family somehow turns a simple visit into a feast at which guests, uninvited as well as invited, are overwhelmed by the abundance of the table and the sincerity of the talk.

Refrigerators, cupboards, pantries, and balconies will be all but emptied to produce a single meal for a visitor, and Russians make a joke of the serious fact that their preparations for that one feast will require a diet of bread and tea for the week to come. A Russian hostess always dreads running out of food, so the dishes on a table set for four could easily feed eight or more. According to an old Russian saying, 'There is never enough food on a table, but always more than enough.'

After climbing up nine flights of decrepit stairs in a once-impressive downtown building, erected in the 1930s and seemingly not tended to since then, my American friend Paul Jones and I caught our breath and rang the doorbell. We could hear giggles and the patter of feet scurrying to the door. Paul's friend Masha, a young, obviously tired mother who volunteers at a theater for disabled children, greeted us. Her two older girls, ages five and seven, hid behind her legs, while her chubby six-month-old baby wriggled in her arms. After presenting our gifts of wine and flowers, we removed our coats and changed out of our boots into slippers kept by the door especially for guests.

This was my introduction to communal apartment life in Moscow. Clothes, junk, and paintings were piled high on both sides of the long, wide hallway. The shared kitchen and dining rooms were off to the right, and the rest of the rooms appeared to be combined living rooms and bedrooms. Because Masha's husband, Mark, an artist, was born in this apartment, the young couple had claim to two of the four large bedrooms. Two single men lived in the other rooms, but they were out for the evening.

Laundry, mostly cloth diapers, hung from a clothesline strung the length of the kitchen. A delicious aroma of vegetable ragout gently simmering on the gas stove filled the air, and I could see a single large red beet boiling in another pot for the classic beet salad with walnuts and garlic.

Meanwhile, the two little girls who had greeted us at the door had changed their clothes, and they came galloping into the kitchen looking like dolls in colorful flowered smocks. Masha explained to us with an innocent, shy smile that tonight was a celebration, not only because we had come for dinner, but because another American friend, Mary, who had also been invited to dinner, had brought them a box of Pampers. It was a banal event by Western standards, but to this Russian family, having Pampers for their baby girl, Anya, was a cause for celebration.

Masha and Mary, friends for several years, had long ago developed a nonsensical, ritualistic exchange to overcome the embarrassment and shock of the striking differences in their living standards that a gift like Pampers revealed. Adopting a line from a poem by Mikhail Lermontov, Mary's response to Masha's involuntary question, 'Where did this come from?' was *'Ot verblyuda,'* 'From a camel,' deeming any attempts to find or afford that particular item ridiculous if not impossible.

We sat down to dinner. Fresh cilantro added the perfect punch to the ragout of vegetables. The shredded beet, walnut, and garlic salad, one of my favorites, and a fresh cabbage salad with vegetables and herbs were exceptionally good. Vegetarian by choice or necessity, this young family had managed to create a tasty and ample meal.

As a worn, scratchy Ella Fitzgerald tape played in the background, I sipped my tea and ate store-bought cookies and Russian chocolates for dessert. The girls were intoxicated by the presence of dinner guests; their parents just wanted to sit and talk all night. Before leaving, Paul and I read, and did our best to translate, Dr. Seuss's *The Cat in the Hat* to the girls, who curled up on our laps.

Brushing off our snow-covered car to go home, I was reminded that a Russian dinner is not just a bounteous meal, but a celebration of companionship, generosity, and the little things in life that bring great joy.

Beet Salad with Walnuts and Garlic

[SALAT IZ SVYOKLY S OREKHAMI I CHESNOKOM]

For centuries, Russians have believed in the healing qualities of red beets. In *The Calendar of a Cook's Garden*, published in 1810, V. A. Levchin writes that the roots and leaves of beets reduce fever, soothe a sore throat, and alleviate headaches. Beets were, and still are, believed to relieve constipation, cure tuberculosis and leukemia, and beautify the skin.

This traditional Russian salad is on the menu of just about every Russian restaurant, but the tastiest versions are to be found in private homes. One of my friends, Lyudmila, whose blond hair and sparkling blue eyes match her cheerful character, cuts her cooked beets very fine instead of grating them, which she insists improves the flavor. She also adds grated dill pickles to give the salad more of a bite. I add a splash of lemon juice.

Many Russians claim that the key to the success of this salad is to use only one very, very large round red beet. Russian beets come in all sizes, from tiny new beets to enormous ones the size of small melons. I have never seen such large beets in the United States, but smaller ones seem to work just as well. For a tasty lunch, I like to serve this salad on a bed of baby greens dressed with a light vinaigrette and garnished with chunks of goat cheese and roasted walnuts. Warm crusty French bread completes the meal.

SERVES 4

1¼ pounds (about 2 large) red beets, washed but not peeled
Sugar
¼ cup chopped walnuts
1 small garlic clove, minced
3 tablespoons high-quality mayonnaise
½ teaspoon fresh lemon juice (optional)
Salt

Place the beets and 1 teaspoon sugar in a saucepan, add enough water to cover, and bring to a boil. Reduce the heat to medium and simmer, covered, until the beets are tender, about 45 minutes. Drain and cool completely.

Peel the beets and coarsely grate into a medium-sized bowl. (Be careful not to stain your clothing with the beet juice.) Add the walnuts, garlic, mayonnaise, and lemon juice, if using, and mix gently. Season to taste with salt, then add a pinch of sugar and mix again. Cover with plastic wrap and let sit at room temperature for 1 hour before serving.

Masha's Vegetable Ragout
[RAGU IZ OVOSHCHEY]

Although we had Masha's vegetable ragout on a snowy day, it is usually prepared during the summer months, when local markets are teeming with fresh produce and fragrant herbs. Treat this adaptation of Masha's recipe as a blueprint – feel free to add or substitute your favorite vegetables and herbs. Vegetables that require a longer cooking time should be added with the eggplant; those that require less cooking with the zucchini. The fresh cilantro, called *kinza*, gives the dish an unexpected kick and should not be omitted.

The ragout can be served hot as a side dish, or at room temperature as a first-course dish. It is lovely over rice or pasta, such as penne or capellini, with freshly grated Parmesan cheese and chopped fresh basil. Thinned with a little tomato sauce, the ragout turns into a delectable base for vegetarian lasagna.

SERVES 8 TO 10

⅓ cup olive oil or canola oil

1 large onion, finely chopped

2 large garlic cloves, minced

3 large carrots, coarsely grated

1 large red bell pepper, cored, seeded, and cut into ¼-inch dice

8 ounces button or cremini mushrooms, cleaned, trimmed, and sliced

1 medium (1 pound) purple eggplant, peeled and cut into ¼-inch dice

4 medium-sized ripe tomatoes, seeded and coarsely chopped, or two 14.5-ounce cans diced tomatoes, drained

1½ teaspoons sugar

Salt

1 cup tomato juice

1 medium zucchini, scrubbed and cut into ¼-inch dice
3 tablespoons chopped fresh parsley
3 tablespoons chopped fresh dill
5 tablespoons chopped fresh cilantro
Freshly ground pepper

Heat the olive oil in a 6-quart heavy-bottomed nonreactive saucepan over medium-high heat until hot. Add the onion and sauté until translucent, about 5 minutes. Add the garlic, carrots, bell pepper, and mushrooms and continue to sauté for 5 minutes, stirring frequently.

Add the eggplant and cook for 3 minutes, stirring constantly to keep the eggplant from sticking. Add the tomatoes, sugar, 2 teaspoons salt, and the tomato juice, mixing well, and reduce the heat to a very gentle simmer. Cook, covered, for 30 minutes. Add the zucchini, stir, and cook until the vegetables are soft and the sauce is slightly thickened, about 30 minutes.

Remove from the heat and add the parsley, dill, and cilantro. Season to taste with salt and pepper. Serve immediately, or let the ragout cool to room temperature, cover, and refrigerate. Bring to room temperature before serving.

Two Russian–Style Cabbage Salads

Cabbage salad *(salat iz kapusty)* is a staple on most *zakuski* spreads (the first course of a Russian meal) and restaurant menus, and there must be hundreds of recipes for it. Salted cabbage (akin to sauerkraut, but slightly less sour than the popular brands in American grocery stores) is sold in large plastic-lined barrels in produce markets, usually next to the pickled vegetables. Many Russians make their own salted cabbage in early fall, using a piece of black bread to start the fermentation process. Russians embellish salted cabbage with carrots, fruits, or nuts, and serve it as a cold salad, or they use it as a base for a popular cabbage soup called *kislye shchi.*

The first of the following two fresh cabbage recipes calls for combining cabbage with carrots in a vinegar-and-oil, or lemon dressing (most Russians use vinegar), while the second mixes cabbage and apples in a sour cream or mayonnaise dressing. Both are simple, tasty side dishes for fish, meat, or poultry. The most important thing to remember when making fresh cabbage salad is to gently crush the cabbage and salt by hand to release the juices and bring out the flavor.

Fresh Cabbage and Carrot Salad with Vinegar-and-Oil Dressing

[VINEGRET IZ KAPUSTY I MORKOVI]

SERVES 4 TO 6

8 ounces white cabbage, tough outer leaves and core removed, quartered, and very thinly sliced

Salt

2 large carrots, coarsely grated

1 tablespoon wine vinegar or fresh lemon juice

3 tablespoons canola oil or olive oil
2 tablespoon chopped fresh dill or parsley
Freshly ground pepper

Place the cabbage in a medium bowl. Add ½ teaspoon salt and mix well by hand, crushing the cabbage to release the cabbage juices, about 1 minute. Add the carrots, vinegar, oil, dill, and salt and pepper to taste and mix well. Adjust the seasoning if necessary and serve immediately.

Fresh Cabbage Salad with Apples and Sour Cream Dressing
[SALAT IZ KAPUSTY S YABLOKAMI I SMETANOY]

SERVES 4 TO 6

8 ounces white cabbage, tough outer leaves and core removed,
    quartered, and very thinly sliced
Salt
1 small apple, peeled and coarsely grated
3 tablespoons sour cream, crème fraîche, or high-quality
    mayonnaise
Freshly ground pepper

Place the cabbage in a medium bowl. Add ½ teaspoon salt and mix well by hand, crushing the cabbage to release the juices, about 1 minute. Add the apple, sour cream, and salt and pepper to taste and mix well. Adjust the seasoning if necessary and serve immediately.

Dinner with a Well-to-Do Russian Family

Besides the usual dinner, consisting of cabbage soup, roast suckling-pig, goose with apples, and so on, a French or 'chef's special' dinner was prepared in the kitchen on major holidays, in case any of the upstairs guests felt like indulging themselves. When the clatter of crockery came from the dining-room, Lysevich began to show visible excitement. He rubbed his hands, twitched his shoulders, screwed up his eyes, and talked with great feeling about the dinners the old men used to give and the superb turbot *matelote* the present chef could produce – more a divine revelation than a *matelote!* He was so looking forward to the dinner, mentally relishing and savoring it in advance. When Anna took his arm and led him into the dining-room and he had drunk his glass of vodka and popped a tiny slice of salmon into his mouth, he even purred with pleasure. He chewed noisily and disgustingly, making curious sounds through his nose, while his eyes became oily and greedy.

– Anton Chekhov, *The Party*

SOON AFTER I ARRIVED IN MOSCOW, I was invited to the home of a well-to-do Russian family with many connections, or *blat* in colloquial Russian. I don't think anyone forgets his or her first meal in a Russian home, especially if the experience involves good food, warm, kind-hearted hosts, and endless vodka toasts.

When I walked into the living room-dining room, I was overwhelmed by the table, which was almost as big as the room and laden with delicacies, the *zakuska* course. This course, I was told by our hostess, should always be laid out on the table before guests arrive – a tradition that dates back to long, horse-drawn carriage journeys and wearied, hungry travelers who needed a bite to sustain them until dinner.

Included among the dazzling array of *zakuski* were a glass bowl filled with homemade pickles and lightly salted cucumbers to accompany the vodka toasts, and a platter of fresh and salted tomatoes with fresh cucumbers resting on a nest of cilantro and parsley sprigs. Small crystal bowls held black and red caviar, and smoked sturgeon was delicately laid out on a platter. The traditional *salat Olivier*, consisting of finely diced cucumbers, apples, and crabmeat, was set out alongside a shredded white radish salad. Thin slices of tangy black bread laced with whole coriander seeds, called *borodinsky khleb*, and white Russian bread were nestled in a basket.

A hearty *borshch* followed the *zakuski*. The black caviar and sour cream were left on the table to garnish the soup. The main course was a simple, traditional village dish – a pork stew with vegetables served in individual covered clay pots. The only trick to making this dish, our hostess told me, is to arrange the meat in the bottom of the pot, followed by the carrots, onions, potatoes, herbs, and spices. Then pop it into the oven for about one hour, long enough for all the flavors to develop and explode in a cloud of steam when the lid is removed.

Dessert was not elaborate: a glass bowl piled high with fresh cherries and a box of Russian chocolates, followed by tea with sliced lemon – a status symbol in Russia that reflects foreign tastes and customs more than Russian ones. Throughout dinner there was a never-ending flow of vodka, accompanied by heartwarming toasts only a Russian can make without sounding foolish – toasts to health, to new friendships, to America, to Russia, and to the future.

This event was the first and only time I dined with the in-laws of my Russian interpreter, Pavel Lebedev. Overwhelmed by the experience of the evening, I quickly lost track of the names of my hosts and most of the other guests, but if you had been a fly on the wall, judging by the warmth and ease of our conversations, you would have thought that we were all lifelong friends. Such is the joy of the Russian table.

The Art of Russian Toasting

Russians are masters of the art of toasting. As the old Russian saying goes, 'In Russia, people do not eat without drinking, and they do not drink without eating.' And they do not drink without toasting! At almost any time of day, even during breakfast hours, a glass of vodka can be raised to offer a toast to seal a business deal, to confirm a new friendship, or to celebrate any one of life's events. For foreigners new to Russia, this ritual can be both charming and alarming.

At some tables, one person, usually the host, is assigned to make all the toasts. At others, toasts are made by every guest. The toaster will usually stand up, hold his or her vodka glass in the air, wait for everyone's undivided attention, and only then begin. People assume great authority on the subject about which they are speaking – and usually no one disputes what has been said. After the toast, the glass of vodka is downed in one gulp, followed by a bite of something salty, usually a pickle, to cut the acid burn. A piece of bread works too.

Some toasts are short and sweet, others ramble on and on. Short or long, they are usually heartfelt and soul warming, on topics ranging from love, peace, and friendship to women, food, literature, and the politics of the day. *'Na zdorovye,'* 'To your health,' is the most common Russian toast, appropriate for all occasions.

Russian-Style Chicken Salad

[SALAT OLIVIER]

Salat Olivier is a Russian salad made famous by a French chef, Monsieur Olivier. M. Olivier, chef to Czar Nicholas II, opened L'Ermitage, a fashionable nineteenth-century restaurant located in Moscow. Originally, this recipe supposedly included grouse, crayfish tails, and truffles. Over the years, the salad has been simplified, and today it is composed of any number of ingredients, including chicken, potatoes, dill pickles, green peas, hard-boiled eggs, and fresh herbs, (although, according to my friend Natalya, onions are never included). Jumbo lump crabmeat or diced cooked shrimp can be substituted for the chicken, and a tart apple, peeled, cored, and diced, can be substituted for the cucumber. I sometimes add diced celery for more crunch, though it is not typically Russian.

SERVES 6

2 large (about 12 ounces) Yukon Gold potatoes, scrubbed
2 large carrots, scrubbed
Salt
8 ounces cooked chicken breast meat, cut into ¼-inch cubes
2 large hard-boiled eggs, diced
1 cup fresh or frozen green peas, cooked, drained, and cooled
2 medium dill pickles, diced
½ cup peeled and diced cucumber
2 tablespoons chopped fresh dill
4 tablespoons chopped fresh parsley
1 cup high-quality mayonnaise
2 tablespoons red wine vinegar
Salt and freshly ground pepper

Combine the potatoes and carrots in a large saucepan, cover

with water, and add 2 teaspoons salt. Bring to a boil and cook just until tender, 20 to 30 minutes. Drain and cool completely.

Peel the potatoes and cut into ¼-inch cubes. Peel the carrots with a paring knife, working around the sides of each carrot, as opposed to the regular top-to-bottom peeling motion. Cut the carrots into ¼-inch cubes.

Combine the potatoes, carrots, chicken, eggs, peas, pickles, cucumber, dill, 2 tablespoons of the parsley, mayonnaise, and vinegar in a serving bowl, and mix gently. Cover with plastic wrap and refrigerate until well chilled, about 2 hours.

Season the salad to taste with salt and pepper, garnish with the remaining 2 tablespoons parsley, and serve. (Any leftovers should be covered and refrigerated.)

My Grandmother's Beet Soup
[BORSHCH MOYEY BABUSHKI]

When you ask a Westerner to name a Russian soup, the most common response is *borshch* – a beet soup of Ukrainian origin, not Russian. Even though *shchi*, a true Russian soup made from fresh or salted cabbage, is undoubtedly the most popular soup in Russia, it is *borshch* that has made a name around the globe.

Of the many different types of *borshch*, I picked this recipe for a Crimean version from my grandmother, Katherine Cheremeteff. She told me that when she lived in the Crimea her mother would start cooking *borshch* at six o'clock in the morning. She would cut all the vegetables by hand, because she claimed they tasted better cut that way. Then she left the soup to simmer all day while she did the housework.

In the traditional manner, my grandmother serves *pirozhki*, popovers filled with meat and hard-boiled egg (page 37), with her *borshch*. This soup is best served on the second day, after the flavors have had a chance to develop. A squeeze of lemon juice and a generous dollop of sour cream, added just before serving, are the perfect foil to the sweetness of the beets.

If you do not want to go to the trouble of making a fresh stock, or if you would like to make this a vegetarian or meatless soup, you can substitute eight cups of canned chicken, beef, or vegetable stock for the stock ingredients. But keep in mind that the key to a truly good *borshch* is a rich stock.

Beef Stock

1½ to 2 pounds beef shank cross cuts

1 large carrot, quartered

1 celery rib, quartered

1 medium onion, quartered

3 bay leaves

7 black peppercorns

1 teaspoon salt

3 quarts water

Beet Soup

SERVES 8

4 tablespoons (½ stick) unsalted butter

1 medium onion, finely diced

2 large red beets (12 to 14 ounces), peeled and coarsely grated

2 large carrots, peeled and coarsely grated

3 tablespoons vinegar (any kind)

8 ounces white cabbage, tough outer leaves and core removed, quartered, and very thinly sliced

1 medium potato, peeled and coarsely grated

¼ cup finely chopped green bell pepper

1½ cups tomato juice or V-8 juice (two 5.5-ounce cans)

Squeeze of fresh lemon juice

3 tablespoons chopped fresh dill

3 tablespoons chopped fresh parsley
Salt and freshly ground pepper
Sour cream, for serving

To make the stock, place all the ingredients in a stockpot, cover, and bring to a boil. Reduce the heat and simmer for 1½ hours, uncovered, skimming as needed.

Remove from the heat and strain the stock into a large heat-proof bowl or clean stockpot. You should have about 8 cups strained stock. Discard the vegetables and save the meat. When the beef is cool enough to handle, remove the meat from the bones and shred it or cut it into small pieces. Set aside.

To make the soup, melt the butter in a large stockpot over medium-high heat. Add the onion and sauté until translucent, about 3 minutes. Add the beets, carrots, and vinegar and continue to sauté for 5 minutes. Add the cabbage and sauté for 5 minutes more. Add the potato and green pepper and sauté for 2 minutes more. Add the stock, tomato juice, and reserved meat and bring to a boil. Reduce the heat and gently simmer, un-covered, for 1 hour, stirring occasionally.

Just before serving, add the lemon juice, dill, and parsley. Adjust the seasoning with salt and pepper to taste and serve immediately. Pass the sour cream at the table.

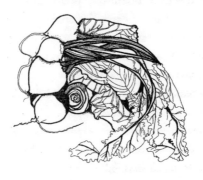

Little Meat-Filled
Russian Pies

[PIROZHKI S NACHINKOY IZ RUBLENOGO MYASA]

I can't give you a recipe for my grandmother's *borshch* without also supplying one for her *pirozhki*. Made with either a yeast dough or a puff pastry-like dough, *pirozhki* are small pastries stuffed with a savory or sweet filling. The savory pastries are usually served with a bowl of soup, such as *borshch* or *shchi*, and they are traditionally filled with boiled beef, double-ground to a pasty consistency. The sweet version, served with tea, is filled with jam or diced fresh fruit combined with a touch of cornstarch to thicken the juices during baking.

Making *pirozhki* always brings back images of my grandmother sitting at her kitchen table in Antigua, a kerchief tied to keep her hair back, gently stuffing little pillows of yeast dough with a meat-and-hard-boiled-egg filling. She would cut off a little piece of the dough for me, and I would play with it contentedly while her fingers, moving effortlessly from muscle memory, would assemble a tray of savory pastries in no time. Then she deep-fried them and neatly arranged them in a cloth-covered picnic basket for us to take to the beach.

Though *pirozhki* are usually eaten with soup, they also make a wonderful hors d'oeuvre or a tasty brunch item.

Yeast Dough

MAKES FORTY 3 1/2-INCH PIROZHKI

One ¼-ounce package active dry yeast

½ cup water, heated to lukewarm (about 100 degrees F)

1 tablespoon sugar

½ teaspoon salt

½ cup whole milk

8 tablespoons (1 stick) unsalted butter

2 large eggs

3¾ cups all-purpose flour, plus flour for the work surface

Meat Filling

4 tablespoons (½ stick) unsalted butter

1 pound extra-lean ground beef

3 hard-boiled eggs, chopped

2 tablespoons chopped fresh dill

2 tablespoons chopped fresh parsley

3 tablespoons finely sliced green onions

½ teaspoon salt, to taste

Freshly ground pepper

Canola oil, for deep frying

To make the dough, combine the yeast, water, sugar, and salt in the bowl of an electric mixer or another large bowl; set aside.

Combine the milk and butter and heat until the butter has completely melted and the mixture is hot. Add the milk-butter mixture and the eggs to the yeast mixture and mix until the yeast has dissolved. Add the flour and using the paddle attachment, mix on medium speed until the flour is well incorporated, about 5 minutes, scraping down the paddle and sides of the bowl as necessary. Or, if mixing by hand, stir the flour into the dough, then turn the dough out onto a well-floured surface and knead until it is smooth and supple. With either method, the dough should be a little sticky. If it is too sticky to work with, add a little more flour, 1 tablespoon at a time. Cover the bowl with plastic wrap and let the dough rise in a warm place for about 1 hour, or until doubled in size.

To make the meat filling, melt 2 tablespoons of the butter in a large nonstick skillet over medium-high heat. Add the beef, crumbling it with your fingers as you put it in the skillet, and cook, stirring occasionally, using the back of a spoon to crumble it very fine, until most of the juices have evaporated and the meat is lightly browned, 7 to 10 minutes. Remove from the heat.

Drain the meat in a sieve, then return it to the skillet and add the remaining 2 tablespoons butter. Place the skillet over medium-high heat and cook for 5 minutes, stirring constantly, until the meat is nicely browned. Transfer to a bowl, and let cool to room temperature.

Add the eggs, dill, parsley, and green onions to the cooked meat, mix gently, and season generously with salt and pepper to taste. The filling should be quite salty. Set aside at room temperature.

To assemble the *pirozhki*, have 2 large dry dish towels ready, and flour a work surface. Dip your hands in flour, pick up the dough, and knead it into a ball on the work surface. Flatten the ball slightly, then, using a floured long knife, cut it into 7 equal strips. Work with 1 strip at a time, keeping both the remaining dough and the assembled *pirozhki* covered with the dish towels.

Using the palms of your hands, gently roll each dough strip into a log about 2 inches thick, then cut it into 1½-inch lengths. Working with 1 piece of dough at a time, lay the dough cut side down on the floured surface and using your hands or a rolling pin, flatten it into a round about 3 to 3½ inches in diameter. Pick up the dough round, place 1 heaping teaspoon of the meat filling in the center, and fold the round in half to form a half-moon shape, then seal the edges of the dough by pinching them together. The dough should be moist enough so that the edges stick together easily. (If not, wet the edges with a bit of water.) Pinch the entire border with your thumb and index finger, then twist the edges over to form a decorative pattern and to seal the *pirozhok* tightly. As you work, set the assembled *pirozhki* aside on a floured work surface, and keep them covered with a dish towel until ready to fry.

To fry the *pirozhki*, line a large platter with paper towels. Heat the oil in a deep-fryer or a wide, deep, heavy-bottomed pot to 350 degrees F. Ease a few *pirozhki* at a time into the hot oil, without crowding them, and, using a slotted spoon or tongs, turn them occasionally as they cook until they are light golden on all sides and the dough is cooked through, about 2 minutes. Remove the *pirozhki* from the oil and drain them on the paper towel-lined platter in a single layer. Transfer to a serving platter and serve warm. (*Pirozhki* can be reheated in a 400 degree F oven for about 5 minutes.)

Russian Cream with Summer Berries
[KREM S YAGODAMI]

Russian cream, served with fresh currants, raspberries, and strawberries that have been quickly sautéed to release their juices, is a light and refreshing dessert. This recipe comes from a British friend, Fiona Black, whose grandmother got it from a Russian friend living in England.

The roots of Russian cream lie in a simple, home-style dessert called *kisel*. Fruit *kisel* is made with cooked fruit to which water and potato starch are added. It can be almost as firm as American Jell-O, or thin enough to drink from a glass. Milk-based *kisel*, which resembles a thin, velvety pudding, is also thickened with potato starch and usually flavored with vanilla or almond extract.

Fiona likes to serve this dessert with a compote of fresh raspberries and red currants. Any mixture of berries, including blueberries, blackberries, raspberries, or strawberries, will work. If you are using frozen berries, thaw and drain off the watery juices before cooking them with the sugar. Do not be tempted to substitute yogurt for the sour cream. It reacts with the gelatin and makes the cream grainy.

Russian Cream

SERVES 6

¾ cup sugar

1 envelope gelatin

½ cup water

1 cup heavy cream

1½ cups sour cream

1 teaspoon pure vanilla extract or other extract, such as orange or
lemon

Berry Sauce

5 to 6 cups fresh berries, cut in half or into quarters if large, or
one 15- to 16-ounce bag frozen berries, thawed and drained

½ cup sugar, or to taste

To make the Russian cream, combine the sugar, gelatin, and
water in a medium-sized nonreactive saucepan, stir, and let stand
for 2 minutes. Place the saucepan over medium heat and bring to
a boil, stirring constantly until the gelatin dissolves.

Remove from the heat and gradually whisk in the heavy cream,
sour cream, and vanilla. Pour into a heatproof serving bowl or
into 6 individual heatproof serving dishes large enough to hold
some berry sauce as well, and refrigerate for at least 8 hours, or
until the cream has set.

To make the berry sauce, combine the berries and sugar in a
large saucepan or skillet and place over high heat. Shake the pan
or gently stir the berries until the sugar has melted and the berries
just begin to give off their juices. Do not overcook; fresh berries
should remain firm. Remove from the heat, cool slightly, and then
transfer to a heatproof serving bowl.

Serve the Russian cream with the berry sauce.

Spring and the Russian Bliny Festival

> They in their peaceful life preserved
> the customs of dear ancientry:
> with them, during fat Butterweek
> Russian pancakes were wont to be.
> – Alexander Pushkin, *Eugene Onegin*

*R*USSIANS BEGIN TO CELEBRATE SPRING well before it arrives. Winters are so hard that even the first partial melting of snow and hint of buds and bulbs is an occasion for replacing a *shapka* (fur hat) with a shawl or scarf, and at least thinking about retiring a heavy coat.

Fresh produce and flowers from Russia's soil reassure its people that spring really is on its way. Moscow's open markets, called *rynki*, come alive in spring. The dark hues of the root vegetables and wilted greens that dominate the stalls most of the year are replaced by heaps of beautiful fresh produce – baby beets, carrots, and strawberries. Buckets of just-picked yellow, white, and cream daffodils, soft calla lilies, rich red tulips, and fragrant hyacinth add to the dazzling display. I was always tempted to buy a whole bucketful of daffodils, and sometimes did. Daffodils are my weakness, perhaps because I was born on the first day of spring, or just because their color and shape cry out, 'Be happy, spring is here, life is beautiful.' And spring is beautiful, particularly after a long Russian winter.

Surviving winter and anticipating spring are occasions enough for celebration, but the Russians have an even greater promise – Easter, and its centuries-old traditions. Before Communism, the festivities of spring and Easter officially began with *Maslenitsa*, Butter Week, *maslo* being the Russian word for butter and oil. Like Mardi Gras, *Maslenitsa* was, and once again has become, the last fling preceding the austerity of the Great Lent before Easter.

During Butter Week, Russians used to gorge themselves on hot *bliny*, yeast-based pancakes that symbolize the golden warmth of the sun. Many still do. Russians eat these pancakes smothered with butter and topped with caviar, smoked salmon, sturgeon, or herring – or, for a sweet touch, with sour cream and fruit preserves. The richness of these pancakes and other indulgences of the table are neutralized and perhaps erased by copious drafts of flavored vodkas – black currant, anisette, lemon, orange, cranberry, paprika, and birch branch (see page 205). Hot tea also aids digestion.

The roots of *Maslenitsa* date back about a thousand years to a pagan festival commemorating the waning of winter and arrival of spring. Centuries ago, Butter Week was celebrated by fairs in all the major cities of Russia. Vendors lined the streets selling hot *bliny*, baked goods, nuts, fish and meat pies, and sweets. Amusement parks with ice slides, monkeys with barrel organs, accordion players, gypsy fortune-tellers, balalaika ensembles, theatrical companies, and clowns all added to the gaiety. Masquerade balls, followed by *troika* rides in the snow, were popular amusements for the rich.

Maslenitsa was a time of such wild merrymaking it was said that people gave their souls to the devil. Despite the pagan roots and riotous revelry of the celebration, the Orthodox Church eventually adopted it, but, in an attempt to minimize the damage, shortened what had been a two-week debauchery to just eight days. A popular greeting during Butter Week remains *'Shirokaya Maslenitsa,'* meaning 'broad,' for the unrestrained pleasure possible during the week.

Today, most of the extravagant Butter Week traditions have disappeared. Friends still gather to enjoy *bliny* and vodka at home, but vendors no longer fill Moscow's crowded streets selling *bliny* hot from the griddle. In a handful of small Russian towns like Suzdal and Ryazan, however, *Maslenitsa* celebrations still take place, and the festivities in the town square are a major social gathering.

In 1993, my friend Paul Jones and I attended the Butter Week festival in Suzdal, an ancient town about three hours from Moscow. As we approached, we found that the roads leading to the center of Suzdal were closed to traffic. We parked our car on a side street and walked into the center of town. The town square had been transformed into a brightly painted stage set for the spring carnival. Vendors, mostly women bundled in furs and colorful Russian scarves, lined the square's edges selling buttery *bliny* wrapped in towels to keep them warm, *oladi* (silver dollar pancakes), *shashlyk*, or shish kebab, *ponchiki* (Russian doughnuts), and assorted sweets all alongside sneakers, used books, a sink, and spare car parts – the consequence of a changing society and tough economic times.

Russians and tourists alike gathered to eat, drink, dance, and share in the gaiety. The townspeople, dressed in colorful traditional peasant costumes – vivid floral-print dresses, shawls, and kerchiefs – and in lively bear and clown costumes, pranced around spreading good cheer. A beautiful snow queen had been elected to preside over the festivities from a throne.

Traditionally, Butter Week festivities officially ended with the burning of a scarecrow, a symbol of the pagan deity who was believed to rule the winter season. Older towns like Suzdal still practice this ritual. In keeping with custom, the straw figure was carried through the town, then set on fire and thrown into the lake.

Everyone shared the hope of warm months to come and abundant crops.

The last Sunday of Butter Week, called Farewell Sunday, is a time for forgiveness and vows to live in peace. If a neighbor or friend has offended you, this is the time for reconciliation. Pots, utensils, and plates are thoroughly cleaned to remove any traces of butter, and houses are blessed in preparation for the seven-week-long Easter fast, the Great Lent.

Butter Week in a Russian Village, 1907

This excerpt, from *The Russian Peasant* by Howard P. Kennard, demonstrates how even the poorest peasants, who would have lived on bread and water most of the year, squandered their savings on the indulgences of Butter Week.

Let us peep at a village during the Feast of *Masslenitsa*. Merrily ring the church bells, and multitudes of sleighs with gaily dressed occupants singing uproariously, and playing the concertina or balalaika, pass to and fro, drawn at the gallop by horses excited by the persuasive cries of the semi-intoxicated drivers. The first four days the villagers keep to themselves, and the feasting, so to speak, goes on at home. The peasant's belly is his God, and he does not cater for guests outside his immediate circle of relations and cronies. He feeds with a vengeance unknown to ordinary mortals. He fairly gives himself up to an orgy of meat and drink during these first four days. Butter is the most prominent delicacy, and is literally absorbed in masses, in view of the fact that for seven long weeks nothing but *oil* must be used instead ... The favorite dish is called *blinni*, a kind of pancake baked in butter and served in a sauce of melted butter.

Every village is gay with the scene. Horses with dignified, leisurely walk pace up and down, drawing their merrily singing occupants; the air is rent with singing, shouts, and salutations, by no means lacking in native wit ... All are in a happy state of alcoholic exuberance.

On Friday night all go to bed to prepare for the two final and most important days of the feast – Saturday and Sunday. On these two days, feasting, driving, dancing, and drinking – especially the latter, reach their height, the amount of vodka consumed ... being enormous. Every *izba* [Russian peasant home] has its table laid with vodka and provisions, and everyone is free to enter and imbibe to the full, to his heart's content.

On Sunday night the orgy approaches to its extreme height. All form circles and dance and drink ... Many are too intoxicated to do anything but roll helplessly and idiotically about ... they are dragged either by comrades less drunk, or else by their female relatives, who, as a general rule, do not partake in such excess.

Pandemonium reigns, and all thoughts of morality, or propriety, or decorum, are thrown broadcast to the winds. All give themselves up to an unbridled bestial orgy, till clang, clang, clang goes the bell, tolling the hour of twelve, the hour ordained by the Church for the feast to cease, and with it the gaiety, the dancing, the drinking – all.

Butter Week Pancakes
[BLINY]

Bliny are very thin, fairly large, porous pancakes that are wrapped around a savory or sweet filling and eaten either as finger food or with a fork and knife, depending on the filling and the rules of the home. They used to be made primarily with buckwheat flour or even rye flour; nowadays, *bliny* are rarely made with anything but white flour.

Traditionally, *bliny* are served only once a year, during Butter Week, immediately preceding Russian Orthodox Lent. During this time, *bliny* are eaten for breakfast, lunch, and dinner, and even at teatime, washed down with hot tea or enough flavored vodka to unclog the arteries.

In my home, *bliny* are made more often. For special breakfasts or brunches, I serve *bliny* with maple syrup, fruit preserves, or fresh fruit. For the truly special occasion, I present them with caviar and thinly sliced smoked salmon with a crème fraîche lime sauce. My mouth waters at the thought!

Bliny are a symbol of the sun – golden, warm, and round. For many Russians, these pancakes hold deep meaning, associated as they are with surviving yet another treacherous Russian winter and with looking forward to spring in all its beauty and bounty. In previous centuries, a single *blin* was placed on the attic windowsill for the souls of the recently departed.

Today, *bliny* parties have become popular both in the city and in the countryside. A Russian hostess usually allows about ten *bliny* for each guest as a savory course, two or three for a sweet serving. Should a *bliny*-eating contest develop, however, *bliny* consumption can increase to twenty-five or even thirty-five per person.

In Russia, a cast-iron skillet is normally kept solely for the once-a-year *bliny*-making ritual. It is never washed with soap and water, only rubbed with rock salt and wiped clean. A large nonstick skillet can also be used with excellent results.

If your first *blin* does not turn out just right, don't despair. As the Russians say, 'The first *blin* is always a lump,' which is a good excuse for the cook to get the first *blin* into his or her mouth, lump or not.

Pancakes

MAKES ABOUT FOURTEEN 8-INCH PANCAKES

1 teaspoon active dry yeast

1 cup whole milk

½ cup water

3 tablespoons sugar

½ teaspoon salt

5 tablespoons unsalted butter, melted and still warm

1 large egg

1⅓ cups plus 1 tablespoon all-purpose flour

1 teaspoon canola oil, for cooking the pancakes

Fillings
Fruit preserves or jam
Sweetened condensed milk
Sour cream
Black or red caviar
Smoked fish, such as salmon or sturgeon

To make the batter, place the yeast in a medium-sized bowl.

Combine ½ cup of the milk and the water and heat to luke-warm (about 100 degrees F). Add the milk mixture, sugar, and salt to the yeast and gently whisk until the yeast has completely dissolved. Add the butter, egg, and flour. Whisk until smooth. Scrape down the sides of the bowl, cover with plastic wrap, and let the batter rise in a warm place for 1 hour.

Stir down the batter, re-cover with plastic wrap, and set aside in a warm place to rise for 30 minutes.

Heat the remaining ½ cup milk to lukewarm and stir it into the batter.

To cook the pancakes, heat the canola oil in a large well-seasoned or nonstick skillet over medium-high heat until hot. Add about ⅓ cup of the batter and immediately swirl the batter to form a thin pancake. Cook the pancake until the surface is firm and the underside is golden brown, about 45 seconds. Turn and continue to cook until the bottom is golden, about 30 seconds. Serve the pancakes immediately. Or, if you are serving them after all the pancakes are cooked, stack them, cover loosely with foil, and place them in a very low oven until ready to serve.

Serve the *bliny* with small bowls of various fillings for people to help themselves at the table. (Any leftover pancakes can be covered and refrigerated. To avoid tearing the stacked refrigerated pancakes when separating them, unwrap the stack and heat in a microwave oven for a few seconds.)

Silver Dollar Pancakes
[OLADI]

These small, thick yeast-based pancakes are served with sour cream, sweetened farmer cheese, fruit preserves, honey, or sweetened condensed milk. In Moscow's center, '*oladi* houses,' small cafeteria-style restaurants, sell these pancakes fast-food style. A machine drops a measured portion of the batter onto a rotating hot grill attended to by a sweaty cook, whose job is to flip and stack the pancakes as quickly as he can. Depending on the season, hot tea or chilled fruit juices are served in these establishments.

Pancakes

MAKES ABOUT TWENTY 3-INCH PANCAKES

½ teaspoon active dry yeast

½ cup whole milk

½ cup water

2 tablespoons sugar

½ teaspoon salt

1 tablespoon canola oil

5 tablespoons unsalted butter, melted and still warm

1 large egg

1½ cups all-purpose flour

1 teaspoon canola oil, for cooking the pancakes

Toppings

Sour cream

Fruit preserves or jam

Honey

Sweetened condensed milk

Farmer cheese, sweetened with sugar or honey

To make the batter, place the yeast in a medium-sized bowl.

Combine the milk and water, and heat to lukewarm (about 100 degrees F). Add the milk mixture, sugar, salt, and canola oil to the yeast and gently whisk until the yeast has completely dissolved. Add the butter, egg, and flour. Whisk until all of the ingredients are well blended. Scrape down the sides of the bowl, cover with plastic wrap, and let the batter rise in a warm place for 1 hour.

Stir down the batter, re-cover with plastic wrap, and set aside in a warm place to rise for another 30 minutes.

Stir down the batter again and proceed to cook the pancakes. The pancake batter will be quite thick and will continue to rise as you cook the pancakes; simply stir it down from time to time. Heat the canola oil in a nonstick skillet over medium-high heat until hot. Add about 2 tablespoons batter per pancake to the skillet, leaving enough space in between the pancakes to turn them. Cook the pancakes until bubbles appear on the surface and the bottom is golden brown, about 45 seconds. Turn and continue to cook until the bottom is golden brown, 45 seconds more. Serve the pancakes immediately. Or, if you are serving them after all the pancakes are cooked, stack them, cover loosely with foil, and place them in a very low oven until serving.

Serve with small bowls of the toppings for people to help themselves at the table. (Any leftover pancakes can be covered and refrigerated.)

Everyday Pancakes with a Sweet Cheese Filling
[BLINCHIKI S NACHINKOY IZ TVOROGA]

Blinchiki are thin, unleavened pancakes, similar to French crêpes, that are served in a variety of ways throughout the year. For a main course, they are cooked on only one side, filled with meat or cheese, and sautéed in butter to reheat before serving. Sometimes they are served stacked, with a savory or sweet filling in between, and then the *blinchiki* cake is warmed in the oven. The cake is cut into wedges and served with soup or tea, depending on the filling.

Blinchiki are most often served with tea, accompanied by jams, fruit preserves, and sweetened condensed milk. In my home, these pancakes are a much-anticipated breakfast staple, served with warm maple syrup or jam. I have also included a recipe for a sweet farmer-cheese filling.

MAKES ABOUT TWELVE 8-INCH PANCAKES

1 cup plain yogurt

1 cup whole milk

2 large eggs

½ teaspoon pure vanilla extract

1 tablespoon sugar

¼ teaspoon salt

¼ teaspoon baking soda

2 tablespoons canola oil

1 cup all-purpose flour

1 teaspoon canola oil, for cooking the pancakes

Sweet Cheese Filling (recipe follows) (optional)

½ tablespoon unsalted butter (if sautéing the filled pancakes)

To make the batter, combine the yogurt, milk, and eggs in a large bowl and whisk until well blended. Add the remaining ingredients and whisk until smooth. Allow the batter to sit at room temperature for 15 minutes.

To cook the pancakes, heat the canola oil in a large nonstick skillet over medium-high heat until hot. Add a little less than ⅓ cup batter to the skillet and immediately swirl the batter to form a thin pancake. Cook the pancake until the surface is firm and the under-side is golden brown, about 30 seconds. Flip the pancake and continue cooking for about 30 seconds, or until golden brown. Or, if you will be filling the pancakes, cook them for only 5 seconds on the second side.

Serve the pancakes immediately. Or, if you are serving them after all the pancakes are cooked, stack them, cover loosely with foil, and place them in a very low oven until serving. (The pancakes can be made up to 6 hours in advance, covered, and left at room temperature before filling.)

To fill the pancakes, lay a pancake golden brown-side up on a work surface. Put about 1½ tablespoons of filling in the center of the lower half of the pancake. Fold up the bottom edge of the pancake just enough to cover the filling, then fold over the right and left sides of the pancake, and roll it up to form a 3½ x 2-inch packet. Place the filled pancakes seam side down on a plate until ready to sauté.

To sauté the filled pancakes, melt the butter in a large nonstick skillet over medium-high heat. Place 4 or 5 pancakes seam side down in the skillet, leaving space to turn them. Reduce the heat to medium-low and cook, turning once, until the pancakes are golden brown and the filling is heated through, about 3 minutes on each side. Transfer the pancakes to a serving platter and cover loosely with foil to keep warm while you sauté the remaining pancakes. Serve immediately. (Leftover filled pancakes can be refrigerated, covered, for up to 2 days. Reheat gently in a skillet over low heat or in a microwave oven.)

Sweet Cheese Filling

Following is a recipe for a plain sweet cheese filling, but feel free to add your favorite flavorings, such as grated orange or lemon zest, jam, marmalade, cinnamon, or extracts. Raisins, currants, dried cherries, or dried cranberries add texture and flavor to this filling.

MAKES ENOUGH FILLING FOR TWELVE 8-INCH
PANCAKES

**12 ounces Friendship All Natural Farmer Cheese, or any slightly
firm, not creamy, farmer cheese**

½ cup heavy cream

2 tablespoons sugar, or to taste

1 teaspoon pure vanilla extract

Combine all of the ingredients in a small bowl and mix until
well blended. Cover and refrigerate until ready to fill the
pancakes. (The filling can be made up to 2 days in advance and
kept, covered, in the refrigerator.)

In the Danilovsky
Monastery Kitchen

During the first two weeks of Lent, it is difficult to cook, and then when you are allowed to use oil you think you can do anything; and then when you are allowed to use fish, you are free, there are no limits to your fantasy. With a little bit of love, any dish can be delicious.

– Galina, the head cook at Danilovsky Monastery, Moscow

TO DISCOVER THE GREAT LENTEN TRADITION TODAY, I visited Moscow's Danilovsky Monastery, one of the city's architectural and historical treasures. Situated on the southeast periphery of Moscow, the monastery served as part of the city's protective ring from the twelfth century to the 1920s, when the Communist Party turned it into a juvenile detention center. In 1983, as a symbol of Soviet President Mikhail Gorbachev's *glasnost*, the monastery was returned to the monks, declared the seat of the Russian Orthodox Patriarch, and restored to its former beauty.

In the monastery kitchen, I met Galina, who cooks for forty-two monks and staff everyday. She is a large, middle-aged woman, with peaceful blue eyes and a soothing voice. Wearing a huge apron and white kerchief, Galina explained the monastery's Lenten and other rules:

During Lent, neither breakfast nor supper is served. The monks eat only one midday meal, without coffee or tea. The only beverages allowed are boiled water with lemon and herbs or *kvas*. All dishes are served cold. No dairy products or sugar may be consumed. Not even fish is served throughout Lent, and meat is never served in the monastery.

A special priest runs the kitchen and decides on the Lenten menu for each day. He has available to him Galina's big green cloth-covered notebook with all her Lenten recipes, including mushroom and cabbage soups, green *borshch* from sorrel or other greens, dried pear soup with croutons, *rassolnik* (pickle soup), wild rice soup, and *pelmeny* (dumplings with potato filling). The day I visited, the monks were dining on lentil-rice soup, bread, fresh fruit, *kvas*, and hot lemon water for their midday meal. Each portion was blessed as it was served to the monks, who were gathered around a large wooden table in the austere dining hall.

Vegetable dishes serve as the main course for all meals. Some of these include boiled, pureed, or baked potatoes; boiled beets, carrots, and turnips; cabbage salad with lemon and salt; radish and cucumber salad; marinated tomatoes; pickled and fresh cucumbers; and vegetable cakes called *shnitsel*. *Kasha*, rice, macaroni, and lentils are served in abundance. At home, Galina, like most of the general population, observes a more relaxed version of these strict Lenten rules.

Galina's eyes lit up as she described the wonderful Lenten cakes she makes using only flour, sunflower oil, water, honey, and yeast. I caught her off guard when I asked if the monastery celebrates the indulgences of Butter Week. Galina chuckled and said, 'Of course, everyone feasts on *bliny*, *tvorog* (farmer cheese), sour cream, and red caviar, when we can get it.'

As Palm Sunday, *Verbnoye Voskresenye*, or Branch Sunday, approaches, vendors gather around churches to sell large bundles of pussy willow branches, a northern substitute for palm fronds. Russians of all ages carry the branches to church to be blessed, and then home to place above icons or in water, to root, so they can be planted later at the gravesite of a loved one.

The week before Easter, called *Strastnaya Nedelya*, or Passion Week (also known as Holy Week), is crowded with preparations for the Easter feast. Families clean house, dye eggs, and prepare delicacies such as *kulich* (Easter bread) and *paskha* (Easter cheese-cake). The custom of dyeing eggs goes back to pagan spring festivals, when eggs were brightly colored to symbolize the rebirth of life. In the Christian tradition, of course, beautifully colored eggs also convey the message of the Resurrection. They are placed around the base of the *kulichi* (plural of *kulich*) on the Easter table and are exchanged as gifts.

For most Russians, dyeing eggs is a simple procedure. Brittle brown onion skins are saved for weeks beforehand. The uncooked eggs are placed on a bed of onion skins in a large pot, covered with water, and boiled until they reach the desired color. The resulting deep brown hue complements the golden crust of the baked *kulich*.

When I entered the kitchen at Danilovsky Monastery, I saw hundreds of white hard-boiled eggs waiting to be colored with paint and beautiful red eggs in flat trays drying off, each tray adorned with a blessed pussy willow. Galina and another cook were sitting behind a large table, each with a bowl of red paint within arm's reach. They smeared their hands with paint, then picked up one of the white eggs and rubbed it until it was covered with an even coat of red.

I asked Galina about the meaning of the eggs for the Church and why they were painted red. 'Like the tomb of Christ,' she told me, 'the eggshell is dead. But inside there is life. And the color red represents the blood of Christ.'

Making *kulich*, the cylindrical dome-shaped, Russian Easter bread, is a form of art. In many homes, recipes have been passed down for decades and logbooks are kept recording *kulich* production every year – which batch succeeded, which failed, and why. Failures are attributed to anything from the weather to the cook's foul mood, to a divorce or death in the family. The mark of a good *kulich*, one Russian friend told me, is not only its taste, but its durability – it must never become moldy and, theoretically, it should last until the next Easter.

At the Danilovsky Monastery, *kulichi* are baked the Tuesday before Easter. Enough are made for every priest and monk, the monastery staff, and friends. When I arrived, about one hundred and fifty yeasty-smelling freshly baked *kulichi* were lined up on a table, covered with brown paper, waiting to be decorated with religious Easter symbols. Three young women in white lab coats and kerchiefs frosted the *kulichi* at long tables in the refectory, piping pink, green, or plain white frosting from plastic bags. Once decorated, these loaves would be blessed by a priest, then distributed to the monks and the staff of the monastery when the fast was broken.

On another table, rows of *paskha*, the Russian Easter cheese-cake, were waiting to be unmolded. The rich, creamy cheesecakes stood draining in ancient four-sided hand-carved wooden molds fastened at the top and bottom with string. Carved wooden molds depicting spring flowers and crosses are rarely used anymore, and most home cooks, myself included, use plastic flowerpots with holes at the bottom for drainage. While the stunning effect of the design-pressed pyramid-shaped *paskha* is lost, the taste is just as delicious.

As snow fell outside, lightly covering the petals of newly blossomed daffodils and hyacinth, the room was filled with the warmth of the *kulichi* and the humming of the women at work creating flower patterns, church scenes, and the traditional XB for *Khristos Voskrese*, meaning 'Christ Is Risen,' on top of the *kulichi*.

Before I left, the kitchen staff gave me a fully decorated *kulich*. We shared it later at home, at our own Easter table, and perhaps because it was made with love by Galina and her colleagues, it tasted heavenly.

Dyeing Eggs with Onion Skins

Natural dyes have been used to color eggs for centuries. One of the oldest methods, which continues to be the most popular in Russia, is dyeing eggs with brittle brown onion skins. The finished product is an earthy, warm brownish-red egg that looks exquisite placed at the base of a golden-crusted loaf of Russian Easter bread. I've also given instructions for the gorgeous marbled eggs Russians create by using bits of onion skin, colored dyes, and a piece of hosiery.

Russians begin saving brown onion skins weeks before Easter. The amount of skins you need depends on the number of eggs being dyed. One dozen will require about four big handfuls of skins. The color of your eggs will depend on how long you leave them in the onion skin-infused water, as well as whether you use brown or white eggs. White eggs are more in demand around the Easter holiday, and their inflated price in Russian markets reflects their scarcity.

To dye eggs with onion skins, arrange the brittle onion skins in the bottom of a large stainless steel stockpot or saucepan. Place the raw eggs on top of the bed of skins, then add enough hot water to cover the eggs. Bring the water to a boil, reduce the heat, and simmer gently for 15 to 20 minutes, or until the eggs reach the desired color intensity. For a more intense shade of brown, bury the eggs under the onion skins while they are cooking. Remove the eggs and place them in an egg carton to dry.

To create eggs with a marbled look, you will need a handful of small bits of dark, brittle onion skins, a pair of neutral-colored (white or beige) pantyhose, and a saucepan of hot water colored with egg dye, prepared according to package directions, or food coloring. Cut the legs from the top of the pantyhose. Tie a tight knot at the toe end of one of the legs. Place a raw egg in the tip of the pouch, add bits of onion skins to cover most of the egg, and then twist the long open end of the stocking around the egg and tie it into a tight knot, exactly as you would tie a knot on a balloon. Cut off the stocking close to the knot. Then tie a knot in the open bottom end of the pantyhose and wrap another egg, just as you did the first, until all of the eggs are wrapped.

Add the wrapped eggs to the colored hot water, bring the water to a gentle boil, and cook the eggs until they reach the desired color, about 15 to 20 minutes. Once the eggs are cooked, remove them from the water and drain them in egg cartons. When they are cool enough to handle, cut open the knots and remove the stockings and onion skins from the eggs. Return the eggs to the egg carton to dry.

Russian Easter Bread

[KULICH]

Kulich, a cylindrical dome-shaped bread, is a symbol of the Russian Easter. It is baked only once a year, and is usually blessed in a ceremony at Church on the Saturday preceding Easter Sunday. *Kulich* is never eaten on the same day it is baked.

For many, baking *kulich* is a very serious affair. Natalya, who shared her recipe with me, has kept a journal of her *kulichi* and *paskha* production over the years. The journal, a yellowing notebook stained by buttered fingers, was actually started by her mother in 1953, 'the year Stalin died,' she adds with a smirk. Her journal entries include the date the *kulichi* were baked and the date of Easter that year, how many she baked, and a summary of her baking results.

When I asked Natalya to share some of her worst memories, she replied with a smile, 'Oh, the memories cause me pain.' Paging through her book, she admitted that in 1974 nothing turned out right because she was in a bad mood. And her grandmother had terrible luck with *kulichi* the year her daughter married, and the year her eldest son divorced his first wife.

Natalya stressed that the most important thing to remember when making *kulich* is to be in a good mood. She added, 'If you are in a bad mood, a pancake comes out instead of a tall, beautiful *kulich*; or the *kulich* will get stuck in the mold.' Besides a good mood, proper kneading makes a good *kulich*. Natalya has never used an electric mixer for kneading her *kulichi*. I give hand-kneading instructions, but I've also adapted her recipe for a standing mixer with a dough hook. Large quantities of dough should be kneaded by hand for at least one hour, or, to quote Natalya, 'until the dough glistens with butter and slides off your hands.' Smaller portions require less time and energy.

Most family members take turns kneading large batches of the dough, switching off about every ten minutes to give tired, red hands a rest. As a reward for their labor, one *kulich* is baked for every member in the family, the size of the *kulich* denoting the seniority of the family member. Coffee cans are commonly used as baking molds, and smaller cans (from canned vegetables) for the younger members of their families. Candied fruits, raisins, nuts, vanilla or almond extract, ground cardamom, or anything else you want can be added to the *kulich* during the last phase of the kneading process. Each loaf can be made with a different flavoring or ingredient or combination.

When the *kulichi* come out of the oven, they are removed from their molds and transferred to a pillow or soft surface lined with a towel. When Natalya bakes *kulich*, she literally tucks the *kulichi* into bed, placing them on a pillow and covering them with a light sheet. When they are completely cool, they are ready to be turned upright and placed on a high shelf out of the reach of impatient hands.

For the Easter feast, a dark orange beeswax church candle is usually placed in the center of the *kulich* and lit before serving. Painted eggs traditionally surround the cake, along with real or paper flowers. Some people decorate their freshly baked *kulich* with a light sugar glaze poured over the top, which trickles down the sides. Even though Natalya never glazes her *kulichi*, I have included a recipe for a *kulich* glaze because glazing is a tradition in my family.

Kulich should be accompanied by *paskha* (page 69), the creamy, crustless no-bake Easter cheesecake, which is spread on a slice of *kulich* like cream cheese on a bagel. To serve the *kulich*, the mushroom-shaped top is cut off first and set aside, then the loaf is sliced horizontally, starting from the top. The top is replaced after each slicing to keep the bread from drying out and to keep the loaf looking its best.

Sponge

MAKES 2 *KULICHI*

Two ¼-ounce packages active dry yeast

¼ cup whole milk

¼ cup water

1 tablespoon sugar

1 teaspoon salt

4 tablespoons (½ stick) unsalted butter, melted and still warm

¼ cup all-purpose flour

¼ cup bread flour

Sweet Dough

12 tablespoons (1½ sticks) unsalted butter

2 large eggs

2 large egg yolks

1 cup sugar

1¾ cups all-purpose flour

1¾ cups bread flour

Unsalted butter, for greasing the molds

Optional Flavoring Ingredients:

    1 teaspoon ground cardamom per loaf

    2 teaspoons pure vanilla or almond extract per loaf

    ¼ cup toasted sliced almonds per loaf

    ¼ cup seedless raisins or dried cranberries per loaf

    ¼ cup diced candied fruit per loaf

    2 teaspoons grated orange zest or lemon zest per loaf

Glaze

1 cup confectioners' sugar, or more if needed

2 tablespoons hot water, rum, brandy, kirsch, or other liqueur, or more if needed

To make the sponge, place the yeast in a large bowl or in the large bowl of a standing mixer.

Combine the milk and water and heat to lukewarm (about 100 degrees F). Add the warm milk mixture to the yeast and gently whisk until the yeast has dissolved. Add the sugar, salt, and melted butter and mix until well combined. Add the flours and mix well with a wooden spoon until all the flour is well incorporated. Cover the bowl with plastic wrap and let rise in a warm place for about 30 minutes, or until doubled in size.

Meanwhile, brown the 12 tablespoons butter. Place the butter in a small heavy-bottomed saucepan and gently simmer over low heat for about 25 minutes, or until the foam has subsided and the butter is a rich golden hue; be careful not to burn the butter. Do not stir. Set aside at room temperature.

To make the dough, combine the eggs, egg yolks, and sugar in the small bowl of an electric mixer (or use a hand mixer) and beat on medium speed until light yellow and fluffy, about 3 minutes. Add the egg-and-sugar mixture to the sponge, and mix with a wooden spoon until combined. Slowly add the browned butter (do not add the dark solids at the bottom of the pan), mixing well, then add the flours and continue mixing until the dough comes together.

To knead the dough by hand, using clenched fists, knead the dough in the bowl (if the bowl is not convenient, turn the dough out onto a lightly floured work surface) until it is glossy from the butter and does not stick to your hands, about 30 minutes. Initially the dough will be a bit sticky; if it continues to stick to your hands after a few minutes of kneading, gradually add up to 6 tablespoons flour, 1 tablespoon at a time. The dough should be smooth, elastic, and glossy. Return to the bowl if kneaded on a work surface.

Or, to knead the dough using a standing mixer with a dough hook, mix on low speed until the dough cleans the sides of the bowl, 10 to 15 minutes. (Periodically check the mixer to make sure the motor is not overheating.) If, after 3 minutes of mixing, the dough is still very sticky, gradually add up to 6 tablespoons flour, 1 tablespoon at a time.

Cover the bowl containing the kneaded dough with plastic wrap and let rise in a warm place for about 1½ hours, or until almost doubled in size.

While the dough is rising, prepare two 13-ounce coffee cans for baking the *kulichi*. Place a can on a piece of parchment paper and draw a circle ½ inch larger in circumference than the base of the can. Cut out the circle, then make ½-inch cuts at 1-inch intervals around the edges of the circle. The piece of paper should fit snugly into the bottom of the can and extend a little up the sides. Next, cut a band of paper to line the sides of the can. Cut a second set of paper liners the same size. Generously grease the inside of each can with butter. Fit the circle-shaped paper liners inside the bottoms of the cans and grease with butter; set aside. Grease one side of the side pieces and set aside to wrap around the dough later.

When the dough has doubled in size, divide it in half. If adding any of the optional ingredients, one at a time flatten each piece of dough on a lightly floured work surface and evenly distribute the ingredient(s) over the surface. Then knead the dough into a ball, tucking in the edges as you knead, until all of the ingredients are well incorporated. Stretch out the ball, wrap it in a reserved buttered side piece, and place the wrapped dough in the prepared can. Gently push down the sides of the dough to create a dome-shaped top. Place the filled cans in a warm place to rise until the dough has doubled in size, about 1 hour.

Position an oven rack one level below the middle position to give the breads room to rise, and preheat the oven to 350 degrees F.

Place the cans in the oven and bake for about 1 hour. To check for doneness, insert a thin wooden skewer in the center of each loaf. The skewer will come out clean when the loaves are ready.

Remove the loaves from the oven and let them stand for 5 minutes, then carefully invert and unmold each loaf. Remove the parchment paper and place the loaves on their sides on a soft pillow or a thick towel lined with paper towels to cool. Once they are cooled, wrap them in foil and store them in an airtight container, or freeze for later.

To make the glaze, place the sugar and water in a small bowl and whisk vigorously until well blended. The glaze should have a slightly thick pouring consistency. If it is too thin, add more confectioners' sugar by the teaspoonful; if it is too thick, add more water, a drop at a time. Slowly pour the glaze over the top of the cooled loaves, allowing it to run down the sides. Set aside, uncovered, to allow the glaze to dry.

To serve the *kulich*, cut off the dome and then slice the loaf horizontally, starting at the top. (Any leftovers should be covered with foil and stored in an airtight container at room temperature. The bread can be made up to a month in advance, cooled completely, wrapped in foil, and frozen.)

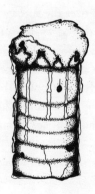

Russian Easter Cheesecake
[PASKHA]

The word *paskha* means Easter in Russian. My mother's luscious, so-good-you-can't-stop-eating-it Easter cheesecake is made only once a year, as an accompaniment to *kulich*, (page 63) the traditional Easter bread. If you don't have the time to make *kulich*, the store-bought Italian Christmas bread (available throughout the year) called *panettone* is a wonderful substitute.

Tvorog, Russian farmer cheese, is traditionally used for *paskha*. In the United States, we do not have an exact equivalent of *tvorog*. Our farmer cheese comes close, but it contains more water than *tvorog*, so it must be drained before the cheesecake batter is mixed, and then again after it is mixed and molded.

Throughout Russia, during the weeks preceding Easter, many small kiosks specializing in religious paraphernalia sell paperback books and pamphlets about traditional Easter dishes, including *bliny*, *kulichi*, and *paskha*. The books contain many recipes, but most of them are outdated and impossible to follow. Some recipes for *paskha* involve cooking or baking the farmer cheese, while others simply call for the fresh cheese to be mixed with hard-boiled egg yolks and molded. Raisins, nuts, and candied fruit are popular additions. Two of my family's favorite additions are candied kumquats (recipe follows) and dried cranberries. Candied kumquats (admittedly not Russian) are simple to make, and they are infinitely more delicate than any packaged candied fruit. Once the *paskha* has been transferred to a serving plate, the base is traditionally decorated with paper or real flowers, colored eggs, or candy.

Cooking Note: Preparation and assembly of this cheesecake requires 2 days.

SERVES 10 TO 12

2 pounds Friendship All Natural Farmer Cheese, or any slightly firm, not creamy, farmer cheese

7 large egg yolks

1 cup sugar

¾ cup heavy cream

4 tablespoons (½ stick) unsalted butter, cut into pieces

1 tablespoon pure vanilla extract

Optional Additions:

  1 cup golden raisins, soaked in ⅓ cup hot water, brandy, or other liqueur for at least 15 minutes to soften, then drained

  1 cup toasted slivered almonds

  1 cup high-quality diced candied fruits or Candied Kumquats (recipe follows)

  1 cup dried cranberries

  2 teaspoons grated orange zest

To drain the farmer cheese, moisten a double thickness of cheesecloth with water, wring it out, and line the inside of a 6-cup flowerpot with it. Place the farmer cheese inside the flowerpot, pack it down, and twist the cheesecloth over the top. Place a small plate just large enough to fit inside the flowerpot directly on top of the farmer cheese, then position a weight (a clean brick covered with foil works well) on top of the plate. Allow the cheese to sit at room temperature for 4 hours; about ¼ cup of water will drain from the cheese.

Combine the egg yolks and sugar in a large mixing bowl and beat with an electric mixer on medium speed until pale yellow and fluffy, about 3 minutes. Transfer the yolk mixture to a heavy-bottomed nonreactive saucepan, add the heavy cream, and set aside. Wash and dry the mixing bowl and set a fine-mesh strainer over it; set aside. Whisking constantly, bring the yolk mixture to a boil over medium heat. This process should take 3 to 5 minutes. Immediately remove from the heat, strain the yolk mixture into the mixing bowl, and cool for 20 minutes.

Gradually add the butter to the yolk mixture, stirring with a whisk until the butter melts. Let cool completely, add the drained farmer cheese and vanilla to the yolk mixture and whisk until well blended, scraping down the sides of the bowl as necessary. Add the optional additions as desired and mix until evenly distributed.

Reline the flowerpot with another double-thickness of moistened cheesecloth, then spoon the *paskha* mixture into it. Fold the edges of the cheesecloth over the top of the *paskha*, place the small plate directly on top of the *paskha*, and position the weight on top of it. Refrigerate the *paskha* for 12 hours, or overnight.

Remove the flowerpot from the refrigerator, remove the weight, and unfold the cheesecloth at the top. Place a serving plate over the top of the flowerpot and invert the cheesecake onto it. Carefully peel off the cheesecloth. Allow the cheesecake to sit at room temperature for 1 hour before serving. Decorate the cake and the serving plate as desired. Serve with slices of *kulich*, or a similar store-bought bread, such as *panettone*. (Any leftovers should be covered and refrigerated.)

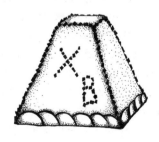

Candied Kumquats

MAKES 1 CUP

2 cups sugar
1 pound small fresh kumquats, washed

Place the sugar and ⅓ cup water in a saucepan and bring to a boil over medium heat. Add the kumquats and return to a boil, then reduce the heat and simmer gently until the kumquats are soft and shrunken and the syrup has thickened, about 1 hour.

Let the kumquats cool slightly, then using a slotted spoon, remove them from the syrup and transfer to a bowl. Using a sharp knife, thinly slice the kumquats, removing any seeds as you come across them. If the kumquats have a lot of pith and membranes, discard the interior and slice only the candied rind.

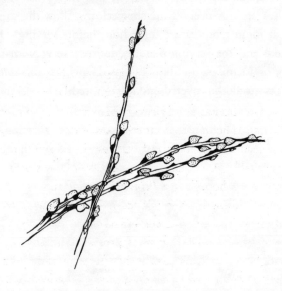

Orthodox Easter Services and an Easter Feast at the Lebedevs'

On Friday the whole house smelled of vanilla and cardamom – the cook had begun baking the Easter cakes. By evening on Mamma's bed a dozen big, tall spongecakes [babas] and squat Easter yeast cakes [kulichi] were laid out under a towel.

> – Aleksey Nikolayevich Tolstoy, from the short story
> 'Passion Week' in *Nikita's Childhood*

FOR RUSSIANS, EASTER IS THE MOST JOYOUS and elaborately celebrated religious holiday. Many Russians who do not attend church all year light a candle and take part in the Easter services, particularly the exquisite midnight mass. The religious and nonbelievers alike engage in Easter's bread-baking and bread-blessing rituals and in the joys of the Easter table. Anticipation during this holiday season is high, and every cook hopes her *kulichi* will be high too.

On the Thursday before Easter 1992, my interpreter, Pavel, invited me to his family's home in Bykovo, a small town about a one-hour drive from Moscow. I went to watch the *kulichi* production – a baking ritual that has sustained the Easter table and Russian spirit over the centuries. Early that morning, Pavel's mother, Natalya, began preparing the *opara* – the yeast and flour sponge that is the first stage in making the bread.

While we waited for the sponge to rise, Natalya told me about her life. Born in Bykovo, she and her family moved to Omsk, in southern Siberia, in 1942 when her father, who could not serve in World War II because of heart problems, was assigned to a factory there. Natalya vividly remembers the three-week train journey to Omsk and the experience of German bombs exploding within yards of the train. The bombs, she said, were aimed at other train cars carrying Russian troops from Siberia to the front.

During her early twenties, Natalya became an enthusiastic *Komsomolka*, or member of the women's branch of the Young Communist League. She worked in a chemical factory in Estonia, and during her free time she wrote for the newspaper, *Komsomolskaya Pravda*. Her articles were so well liked that she was invited to attend the *Komsomolsky* School of Journalism in Moscow.

In 1961, upon graduating, Natalya moved to Kazakhstan, where, she said, 'Khrushchev was on a corn-growing campaign, sending thousands of people there to work in the fields. He also wanted to build a culture down there and he needed journalists to create a newspaper.' During her three years in Kazakhstan she met her first husband, who was on a similar mission, and had her first son, Sergey. Soon after she moved back to Moscow, her marriage fell apart. She remarried, to a childhood sweetheart, and had two more sons. Natalya retired after twenty-nine years of editing, and when I met her, her favorite activities were traveling with her choir group to European cities, sharing a table with friends, and taking care of her grandchildren.

We lost track of time chatting, and when we checked the sponge, it had more than doubled in size. Natalya added some ingredients to the bowl. Then her husband, Yevgeny, kneaded the dough by hand for one hour; this had been his duty since their marriage. He started the process with a smile, but as time went by, his glances at the clock became more frequent, and when the hour had finally passed, he sighed with relief as he cleaned his red, over-worked hands. Natalya left the dough to rise for about two hours, and then she placed it in greased tin cans, like coffee cans, for a final rise before baking. As it baked, she took a rest and prayed for tall, beautiful *kulichi*, not 'flat pancakes.'

In most Russian homes, *kulichi* are baked and preparations for *paskha*, the Easter cheesecake, are made on Clean Thursday, a day traditionally devoted to cleaning the house and baking. Some families choose to bake, to make their *paskha*, and to dye eggs the next day, Good Friday. In either case, these Easter treasures must be ready by Saturday morning, when family members carefully wrap their *kulichi*, *paskha*, and dyed eggs in embroidered towels and carry them to church to be blessed.

To see this Easter food-blessing tradition, I ventured back to Danilovsky Monastery, where I had learned about the Great Lenten tradition from Galina, the monastery cook. Snow flurries that morning did not deter the crowd that had brought their Easter treasures to church. Daffodils, tulips, and hyacinth also defied the weather. In the monastery courtyard, dozens of women and men of all ages, and children too, stood in a long line waiting for a spot on the table. They carefully unpacked their bundles and meticulously arranged their Easter goods on embroidered cloths or on plates. Most people inserted a single beeswax church candle into the dome of each *kulich* and surrounded the base of the bread with eggs, real or paper flowers, and pussy willow branches. Some placed the candle on their *paskha*.

As the priest approached each offering, the candles were lit, and people hunched over the table, protecting the flames from the sharp wind with cupped hands. Holding a bowl of holy water and a brush, the priest walked the length of the table, sprinkling the food and the people with a shower of holy rain that extinguished the candles. People responded to the priest's continuous chanting with prayers, and by making the sign of the cross three times.

Once their delicacies had been blessed, people quickly wrapped them up, and each vacant spot was filled by the next person in line. With midnight service only hours away, people hurried home to finish their last-minute preparations for the Easter feast. The priest repeated his rounds until every bundle of Easter food in the courtyard had been blessed.

By ten o'clock that evening, throngs of people had reconvened on the grounds of the monastery. The evening air was light and crisp, and the snow had ceased. The stars sparkling above mirrored the candles flickering below, held by hundreds of hushed worshippers. Inside the church, candles glowed in front of gold-framed icons, creating dazzling reflections. The air was sweetened by incense, and the melodious chants of the choir reverberated in the vaulted domes. The anticipation was contagious.

As devout old *babushki* (*babushka* is the familiar name for a Russian grandmother, but it is also used to describe any older woman who looks as if she could be a grandmother), their heads covered by scarves, prayed before icons, people busily scribbled special intentions on little slips of paper at the back of the church. Long lines formed for the purchase of icons, prayer books, and candles to be lit at the midnight hour. As midnight approached, most of the crowd inside the church slowly moved outside. Some worshipers with a special invitation *(propusk)* and the infirm were allowed to remain inside, and they moved to the front of the church to secure their places for the service.

The crowd outside formed a circle around the church, clearing a path for the ceremony in which the clergy walk around the church as if searching for the Savior's body. Tapers were lit, and the flames passed from person to person, just as faith in Christ is passed from one person to another.

When the church bells tolled midnight, the doors of the iconostasis (the wall of icons separating the worshipers from the high altar) were thrown open and the representations of the tomb and cross removed. The priests and their male attendants, all clad in colorful gold-brocade vestments, stood at the head of the stairs holding crosses, banners, and tapers. They descended into the sea of flickering lights, chanting and swinging censers, which perfumed the air with incense as they walked around the church three times.

After making three full circles, the priests climbed the stairs and one of them joyously announced three times, *'Khristos Voskrese'* ('Christ Is Risen') to which the crowd joyously responded, *'Voistinu Voskrese'* ('He Is Risen Indeed'). People were exuberant, their faces glowing in the candlelight. Families and friends exchanged triple kisses, hugs, and verbal greetings as the clanging of the church bells filled the air.

Inside the church, the priests and choir continued to chant, *'Khristos Voskrese,'* with the parishioners answering, *'Voistinu Voskrese.'* The service continued for about three more hours. The intense atmosphere inside was dizzying, and several people fainted. The crowd outside the church, however, had dispersed almost immediately after the procession ended. People hurried home to warmth and to break the fast with a small bite or a full-blown feast.

For the priests at Danilovsky Monastery and for many Orthodox Christians, the Great Lent is usually broken by a small meal. Galina explained that at four o'clock on Easter morning, the priests and invited guests sit down to colored hard-boiled eggs, fish sandwiches, potato puree with butter and milk, *kasha*, cheese, and omelets made only from egg whites. The yolks would have been used earlier in all the Easter baking and cheesecake preparations. Cocoa and tea are drunk with much delight after seven long weeks of only hot water with lemon and herbs.

After this short break, both the priests and numerous parishioners return to church for the seven o'clock service. Only after the second service do the clergy and many Russians truly indulge in their Easter feasts. The monastery's Easter menu usually includes consommé with fish, hard-boiled eggs, potatoes fried with fish, fish in wine sauce, hot and cold sturgeon, fish in aspic with horseradish, red and black caviar, *salat Olivier*, a tossed green salad with a vinaigrette dressing, fresh tomatoes and cucumbers, butter and sour cream, fruit syrups, and, of course, the blessed *kulich* and *paskha*.

The Lebedev family invited me back to Bykovo to share their Easter celebration. I was greeted at the door by triple kisses and the words, *'Khristos Voskrese.'* Fresh calla lilies and irises on the dining room table were surrounded by platters of smoked fish on sautéed black bread rubbed with garlic, salted herring with onions, beet salad, cucumber and egg salad, *satsivi* (a Georgian chicken salad), sautéed chicken legs with fresh herbs (referred to as 'Bush legs' because they were part of a U.S.-sponsored food shipment!), boiled potatoes, and a bowl of hot chicken consommé. The meal ended with piano playing and singing. Tea was served with the rich *paskha*, buttery golden *kulich*, and a classic Russian-style apple pie.

It is the custom to have an egg fight at the Easter table, and our table observed it. At the end of the meal, each of us picked up a hard-boiled egg and turned to face our neighbor. When a signal was given, each person held his or her egg as tightly as possible and tapped his neighbor's. Most eggs crack during the first round, but the game continues until only one egg remains whole, its shell intact. The victorious egg rests on the table, while the cracked eggs are consumed immediately or saved for breakfast.

Radonitsa (derived from the word *radost*, or joy), is a ritual that officially takes place on the ninth day after Easter Sunday, a Tuesday, although many Russians also celebrate the rite on Easter Sunday or Easter Monday. *Radonitsa* is a time when Russians visit the gravesites of their loved ones to express and share the joy that embraces the paschal season. Fenced-off graveyard plots, complete with wooden benches and concrete tables and chairs, become intimate gathering places. Relatives and friends clean, then decorate the graves with wreaths of plastic flowers, fresh flowers, plants, and blessed pussy willow branches. It is a common sight to see relatives and friends partying at the gravesite with picnic baskets and vodka – but never clinking glasses, which tradition forbids. Russians believe sharing food, a toast, and happy moments with a departed loved one at the gravesite is a means of keeping that person's spirit alive in the hearts of those left behind. They also leave food for the departed – Easter eggs cracked open, bits of kulich, sausages, pickles, and candy. This becomes a feast for the birds, particularly the crows that hover overhead like a noisy black cloud.

The paschal season, having begun with the indulgences of *Maslenitsa* (Butter Week), followed by almost two months of fasting, then feasting again, comes to a close with the Feast of the Ascension, forty days after Easter. For Russians, the Orthodox Easter is a celebration that honors Christ's Resurrection, nature's renewal, family, beauty, faith, and joy – truly, in all its parts and as a whole, a feast of life.

Carrot, Beet, and Potato Salad
[VINEGRET]

This pink-hued salad is one of the highlights of the Russian *zakuski* spread. The sweetness of the beets and carrots is balanced by the earthiness of the potatoes, with the dill pickles providing the perfect tang and crunch. Keeping the right proportions of these vegetables is essential to the true Russian flavor.

Even though the name, *vinegret*, suggests a vinegar-based dressing, no vinegar is used in this salad. Oil or mayonnaise is the traditional dressing, and it is sometimes served separately at the table so that each person can dress his or her own salad.

This recipe is the most traditional version of *vinegret*. Some people, like my mother, add hard-boiled eggs and green peas. When my mother serves her so-called Russian salad, she mounds it in a serving bowl, smoothes the top with a thin layer of mayonnaise, and then decorates the surface in geometric patterns using an array of finely minced ingredients including beets, carrots, hard-boiled egg whites and yolks, and parsley. She uses thinly sliced pickles or peas to form rows and borders. The effect is stunning, and guests are always hesitant to serve themselves, lest they destroy her masterpiece.

SERVES 4 TO 5

3 small red beets (6 to 8 ounces), washed but not peeled
2 medium potatoes (6 to 8 ounces), washed but not peeled
2 large carrots, washed but not peeled
3 medium dill pickles, cut into small dice
½ teaspoon sugar
¼ cup olive oil or ½ cup high-quality mayonnaise
Salt and freshly ground pepper
2 tablespoons chopped fresh parsley, for garnish

Place the beets, potatoes, and carrots in a large saucepan, cover with water, and bring to a boil. Cook the carrots for about 15 to 20 minutes, the potatoes for about 30 minutes, and the beets for about 40 minutes (the cooking times will depend on the size of the vegetables), removing each vegetable as it is cooked; drain and cool.

Peel the beets and potatoes, cut into ¼-inch cubes, and place them in a medium bowl. Peel the carrots with a paring knife, working around the sides of each carrot, as opposed to the regular top-to-bottom peeling motion. Cut the carrots into

¼-inch cubes and add them to the beets and potatoes.

Add the pickles, sugar, and oil and mix gently. Adjust season-ing to taste. Cover with plastic wrap and refrigerate until well chilled, about 2 hours.

Adjust the seasoning, garnish the salad with the parsley, and serve. (Any leftovers should be covered and refrigerated.)

Chicken with Walnuts, Garlic, and Fresh Cilantro
[SATSIVI]

Satsivi is a Georgian dish whose name literally means 'eaten cold.' There are hundreds of recipes for chicken *satsivi*, and while all of them vary a little, the four main ingredients never change – chicken, walnuts, garlic, and fresh cilantro. This dish is usually accompanied by Georgian flat bread, called *lavash*, to soak up the sauce, but any hearty bread is fine. I like to serve chilled chicken *satsivi* with bread and the hot version with a grain such as couscous or rice. A fresh green salad on the side makes a perfect meal. The walnut and cilantro garnish is essential for the flavor and texture.

Chicken and Stock

SERVES 6 TO 8

One 3- to 3½-pound chicken
1 small onion, cut in half
3 parsley sprigs
3 bay leaves
7 black peppercorns
2 teaspoons salt or 2 chicken bouillon cubes
About 2 quarts water

Walnut Sauce

½ cup sour cream

4 cups reserved chicken stock (from above)

1 cup chopped walnuts

1 cup tightly packed fresh cilantro leaves

½ teaspoon salt

3 tablespoons unsalted butter

1 large onion, finely chopped

1 garlic clove, minced, or to taste

1 teaspoon ground coriander

½ teaspoon paprika

¼ teaspoon cayenne, or to taste

3 tablespoons quick-dissolving flour, such as Wondra, or more as needed

½ cup chopped walnuts, for garnish

⅓ cup chopped fresh cilantro leaves, for garnish

To cook the chicken, combine the chicken, onion, parsley, bay leaves, peppercorns, and salt in a large pot. Add enough water to completely cover the bird and bring to a boil, skimming the foam as necessary. Reduce the heat to medium and simmer, uncovered, until the chicken is tender, 1 to 1½ hours.

When the chicken is cooked, remove it and set it aside to cool. Strain the stock, and measure out 4 cups; refrigerate or freeze the rest for another use. Rinse out the pot and set it aside to make the sauce.

When the chicken is cool enough to handle, remove and discard the skin and bones and tear or cut the meat into small pieces. Place the chicken in a bowl, cover, and set aside at room temperature.

To make the sauce, combine the sour cream, ½ cup of the chicken stock, the walnuts, cilantro leaves, and salt in the bowl of a food processor and pulse to a thick puree. Set aside.

Melt the butter in the rinsed-out pot over medium-high heat. Add the onion and sauté until light golden brown, about 5 minutes, stirring frequently. Add the garlic and sauté for 30 seconds more. Add the coriander, paprika, cayenne, and the quick-mixing flour and cook, stirring constantly, for 30 seconds. Add the remaining 3½ cups chicken stock, whisking constantly, and bring to a boil, then reduce the heat to medium and simmer for 2 minutes.

Stir in the walnut purée and continue to simmer for 5 minutes, then add the chicken and simmer for 5 minutes more. The sauce should be the consistency of a thin gravy; it will thicken as it cools. (If you are serving this dish hot, feel free to add more quick-mixing flour to reach the desired consistency.) Remove from the heat and allow to cool to room temperature, then cover and refrigerate until slightly chilled, about 3 hours.

To serve, remove the chicken *satsivi* from the refrigerator and let it sit at room temperature for about 1 hour. Adjust the seasoning, transfer the *satsivi* to a large serving bowl, and garnish with the walnuts and chopped cilantro.

Two Kasha Recipes

I like it as it comes from the pot, hot with butter or sour cream, and it is one of my daughter's favorite meals, cold in a bowl with cream and brown sugar. I like it mixed slightly with hot sliced mushrooms, or under mushrooms in a sharply seasoned sour cream. I like it alongside any gamey meat, from venison to sauerbraten, in or near or quite without a sauce. It seems that I like it.

– M. F. K. Fisher on *kasha*, from *An Alphabet for Gourmets*

Russians cannot live without *kasha*. It holds such a prominent place in their food world that it is the subject of many jokes and colloquial expressions. My favorite is, 'He's got *kasha* in his head,' which means he's confused.

These toasted buckwheat groats are a dietary staple that have been around for centuries and will probably never disappear. The slightly sweet, earthy smell of *kasha* cooking on the stove or in the oven reminds me of my friend Natalya, a true fan of *kasha*. She makes a big pot of it every Monday and reheats it in a frying pan as needed throughout the week. Like many other Russians, Natalya eats *kasha* almost every morning, with butter, warm milk, and sugar.

Kasha can be prepared and served in countless different ways: boiled, sautéed and then boiled, baked in a casserole or in a pumpkin shell, or mixed with fruits or vegetables. As with rice, once the saucepan is covered, *kasha* should never be stirred. My mother insists that if a bit of baking soda is added to the *kasha* two minutes into the cooking process, the grains won't lose their reddish color.

In both of the following recipes, I use whole *kasha*, not the coarse, medium, or fine grains which tend to turn to mush when cooked. With its distinctive, nutty flavor, *kasha* is a great side dish for meat, poultry, or fish, and a versatile grain for vegetarians. For Russians, any form of *kasha* is comfort food.

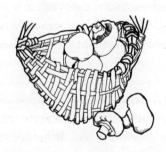

Kasha with Mushrooms, Leeks, and Walnuts

[KASHA S GRIBAMI, POREYEM I OREKHAMI]

SERVES 4

2 tablespoons unsalted butter

½ cup whole *kasha* (buckwheat groats)

1 small leek, washed thoroughly and thinly sliced, or 1 small onion, finely diced

4 ounces mushrooms (any kind) cleaned, trimmed, and thinly sliced

1 cup water or stock

½ teaspoon salt

⅓ cup chopped walnuts or hazelnuts, toasted

Melt the butter in a large nonstick saucepan over high heat. Add the *kasha* and sauté for 2 minutes, stirring occasionally. Add the leeks and mushrooms and continue to sauté for 3 minutes, stirring occasionally.

Add the water and salt and bring to a boil, cover, then reduce the heat to low and cook until the grains are tender, about 10 minutes. Be careful not to overcook the *kasha*, or it will turn to mush. Let sit for 5 minutes before serving.

Sprinkle the *kasha* with the walnuts and serve immediately.

Kasha with Dried Cranberries and Toasted Almonds

[KASHA S KLYUKVOY I MINDALYEM]

SERVES 4

2 tablespoons unsalted butter

½ cup whole *kasha* (buckwheat groats)

⅓ cup dried cranberries

1 cup water

⅓ cup toasted sliced almonds or other nuts

Melt the butter in a nonstick saucepan over high heat. Add the *kasha* and cranberries and sauté for 2 minutes. Add the water and bring to a boil, then reduce the heat and simmer, covered, for 10 to 15 minutes, or until the *kasha* is tender. Be careful not to overcook the *kasha*, or it will turn to mush. Let sit for 5 minutes before serving.

Sprinkle the *kasha* with the toasted almonds and serve immediately.

Tea with Antonina in Strogino

> 'Twas growing dark; upon the table, shining,
> there hisses the evening samovar,
> warming the Chinese teapot;
> light vapor undulated under it.
> Poured out by Olga's hand,
> into the cups, in a dark stream,
> the fragrant tea already ran,
> and a footboy served the cream.
> – Alexander Pushkin, *Eugene Onegin*

NOTHING COULD BE MORE IMPERSONAL AND degrading, nothing could display more clearly the old Soviet Communist contempt for the individual, than the seemingly endless sprawl of faceless high-rise apartment buildings surrounding Moscow. All seem alike – concrete gray, littered, defaced, and broken.

To drive out of Moscow from the center, moreover, is to endure traffic that seems equally contemptuous of life and courtesy. Taxi drivers in dirty yellow Volgas swerve from lane to lane as if they do not care whether anyone lives or dies, and pedestrians stride off the curb into the danger of the street, as if they, too, have left all to fate.

But over the centuries Russians have learned – and fortunate visitors learn, as well – that the kindness and comforts of home, even the smallest room, can compensate for all the insults of the street. And within the home there is perhaps nothing as reassuring as the custom of having tea.

Late one afternoon in August, my friend Antonina invited my mother, my sister, Elizabeth, and me to have tea with her and her daughter, Larissa. We drove forty-five minutes to Strogino, a suburb on the outskirts of Moscow along the Moscow River.

The building was typical – the entry dark and dirty, the paint on the walls chipped, and the word 'anarchist' (in English) sprayed opposite the rusted mail boxes. The gray concrete stair-well smelled of rotting garbage and worse, and the stair railing had been twisted into a useless coil – probably by young hoodlums, whom the Russians call *khuligany*.

When you visit anyone in Russia, it is the custom to bring an odd number of flowers – even one wilted carnation. So, laden with fresh flowers, sugar, coffee, and other scarce tributes, we climbed the cold stairs to apartment number 6 and rang the bell. Immediately, loud barking came from within, and then an attractive older woman and her brown poodle greeted us: Antonina and Dar.

The yeasty smell of pies baking filled the air and we were embraced immediately by light and warmth. The stress and dreariness of the rush-hour trip was dissolved almost at once by the calm of Antonina's private world. We entered a two-room apartment, plus kitchen, in which three people live – the two living rooms doubled as bedrooms at night. Contemporary art and bookcases filled almost every inch of the walls, and hundreds of books, especially art books, lined the shelves. A complete collection of Lenin's works was hidden on a corner shelf.

We sat in the living room at a large table covered with a white linen tablecloth and adorned with a splendid array of sweet and savory pastries. At one end of the table there was an electric samovar, and on top of it was the teapot in which the tea was brewing under a tea cozy shaped like a traditional Russian *babushka* (grandmother).

Highlighted against the white tablecloth, long-stemmed crystal bowls resembling cupped champagne glasses were filled with various fruit preserves, or *varenye:* raspberry, apricot, cherry, and plum *varenye* glistened like precious stones. Delicious savory pies, including cabbage-and-hard-boiled-egg, rice-and-mushroom, and *shchavel,* or sorrel, pie, were served in such abundance that our tea could have been a full meal. Apricot *pirozhki,* or turnovers, and *vatrushki,* pastries similar to cheese-filled Danish, were the perfect sweet touch.

A choice of Chinese black tea or mint tea was offered. Antonina, our hostess, poured some concentrated tea from the teapot into our cups, then filled the cups with boiling hot water from the samovar. Small crystal bowls, called *rozetki,* were provided at each place setting for the *varenye.*

My mother, sister, and I still relish our first tea with Antonina and all the traditions we encountered in her cozy apartment. On subsequent visits to Strogino, as I got to know Antonina a little better, we would sit down to a cup of tea at the kitchen table, where, she said, 'special guests are served and special conversations take place. The kitchen,' she explained, 'is the soul of the house where all the warmth flows from.'

One frosty winter day, as we huddled at the kitchen table sipping tea, Antonina shared her past with me. During World War II, she served in the Russian army as a lieutenant in the medical section of a motorized rifle brigade of the Second Army of Polish Forces. She met her future husband on a train headed from Poland to Siberia. Smitten by her beauty, the young officer approached her. They chatted until the train reached Moscow, where he got off. He asked if she would stay in Moscow, but she declined the offer and continued her journey. A few weeks later, she received a letter from him, which she shared with me – her warm smile recalling the tenderness of her first and only love, while her glistening eyes registered the dark pain of loss. They eventually married and at the age of forty-two her husband died of a heart attack, leaving Antonina with a young daughter and an emptiness in her life that has never been filled.

Antonina said that she tries to start her day with a swim in the Moscow River, a ritual she performs well into October, and spends the rest of her time taking care of the poodle, Dar, her daughter, and her son-in-law, who, she says, will never leave his wife because 'he adores my cooking too much.' Walking around the kitchen in her bare feet, which she insists 'allows the bad energy to leave the body,' Antonina not only introduced me to the spiritual ritual of tea, but became for me a symbol of the Russian people. She had known war when she was eighteen. She had seen Warsaw burning and hungry children hiding in basements. She had lost the only man she had loved. But she remained patient, generous, and kind – her two little rooms are an island of warmth and endurance.

Russian Samovars

For Antonina and other Russians, the samovar is a symbol of family, home, comfort, and friendly communication. Young couples are still given a samovar as a wedding gift, as a good omen that they will lead happy lives together. The samovar's design encourages sustained conversation, because when the samovar boils, the hostess does not have to leave her guests to go to the kitchen. She simply pours the boiling water into the teacups at the table.

The name *samovar*, literally translated as 'self-boiler,' is derived from two Russian words, *sam*, meaning 'itself,' and *varit*, meaning 'to boil'. Traditional samovars, made of copper or brass lined with tin, have a tube running down the center in which pinecones, used to perfume the water, and small pieces of wood and charcoal are burned. The samovar gets so hot it can boil water and keep it hot for hours. A spigot, usually on the front of the samovar, releases a flow of water.

It is difficult to say exactly when, or from where, the first samovar appeared in Russia. But by the middle of the nineteenth century, according to a Russian book called *Russian Samovars*, three basic types of samovar existed: the 'samovar kitchen,' which featured a lot of different compartments for different purposes, such as boiling eggs or making *kasha*; the 'coffee samovar,' which had a special frame inside it with a canvas sieve placed in it to make coffee; and the 'travel samovar,' which was used primarily to boil water both in the home and outdoors at picnics, parties, or on long journeys. It is this last design that has survived the test of time.

Samovar production started near the copper mines in the Ural Mountains. By the end of the nineteenth century, Tula, a town located about 110 miles south of Moscow that became famous for manufacturing armor, was the center of samovar production in

Russia. Each factory in Tula produced its own style of samovar, and each producer stamped a seal of authenticity on the samovar's base. These stamps are still in use.

Different nicknames have been given to the samovar over the years. It used to be called 'golden samovar' or 'golden Ivanovich,' Ivanovich being the patronymic for the most popular Russian name, Ivan, or John. In the 1920s and 1930s, during Stalin's reign, *samovar* was used as a colloquial term for an excellent worker.

The samovar has always been an essential item for Russian travelers. On Russian trains, every passenger car is equipped with a large samovar. Shortly after the train pulls out of the station, the train monitor, usually a tough, buxom woman, bangs on your compartment door to inquire if you'd like some tea. For a small price, tea is brought to you in the traditional metal filigree glass holders, used centuries ago as part of the 'traveling samovar' kit.

Today there is at least one samovar in almost every Russian home – usually two, an electric one for daily use and a traditional one for decoration or for use outdoors at a summer *dacha*. Both are reminders of the essential place of tea in Russian life. A stimulant, a bond, a refreshment, tea is an enduring symbol of the personal and emotional qualities that no hardship or tyrant has ever destroyed.

Russian Tea Through the Ages

> One young humorist sipped his tea through a lump of sugar and
> kept saying, 'Sinner that I am, I love to spoil myself with the Chinese
> Herb.' Now and then he sighed deeply as he asked, 'Please, just one
> more little dish-full.' He drank a lot, noisily crunched his sugar,
> thinking this was all very funny and original, and that he was giving
> a superb imitation of a merchant.
>
> – Anton Chekhov, *The Party*

Though the origins of tea in Russia remain a mystery, consumption throughout the last century remained high among all
ages and economic backgrounds. My Russian friends were all
eager to give me their own theories of how, when, and where tea
first appeared in Russia, but the most well-documented and
plausible account of tea's history in Russia comes from Robert
Smith's 'Whence the Samovar?' an essay in a journal called *Petits
Propos Culinaires*.

When tea from Mongolia first appeared in Russia, sometime
during the seventeenth century, it was greeted with skepticism.
The earliest tea, commonly referred to as 'caravan tea,' resembled
a porridge-like substance, made from brick tea (inferior-quality
black tea that was placed under high pressure to shape it into
bricks), that was crumbled into milk, mixed with grain and
butter, and heated in a Chinese hot pot. It was consumed as a
meal-and-beverage-in-one by tea traders along trade routes over
land.

Toward the end of the seventeenth century, increased imports
of tea into Western Europe caused the price of tea to fall
sufficiently for it to become a popular drink there. According to
Robert Smith, lower tea prices, combined with the interruption of
the tea trade over land due to the closing of a central trading post
in K'achta (a small town near the Mongolian border below Lake

Baikal), and strained relations with the Chinese, resulted in the exporting of tea from Western Europe to Russia by sea. The Russians caught on to the quicker, cheaper, and more efficient sea trade, and by the late nineteenth century, once difficulties with China were settled, regular tea shipments were arriving in Odessa, a southeastern port, and Vladivostok, in the northwest, directly from China. By this time as well, tea plantations were fairly well established on Russia's southern soil, particularly in Georgia and Azerbaijan, but the quality was considered poor and the tea had to be mixed with imported tea leaves.

By the reign of Catherine the Great (1762–1796), tea drinking became popular among the nobility and landed gentry of Russia. Among the privileged class, tea was a status symbol, a luxury item that distinguished the rich from the masses. A century later, when tea was truly affordable and readily available, the ritual of drinking tea became an institution among all social classes and tea replaced *sbiten*, a low-alcohol honey-herbal drink brewed at home and on the streets, as the national drink of Russia. At the same time, the traditional Russian samovar became more commonplace, and it replaced the portable flask-like device used to keep *sbiten* warm.

Throughout the nineteenth century, members of the Russian aristocracy hosted enormous tea parties, both indoors and out, to which hundreds, sometimes thousands, of guests were invited. After large balls, at around two or three o'clock in the morning, a tea buffet would be laid out for guests before they departed. Imported French chefs and their brigades spent days in the kitchen preparing *petits fours* and other pastries and sweets for these events.

But for the average Russian, tea was a simple custom in the home, as it is today – a ritual practiced two or three times a day, usually once in the morning and once or twice in the evening. All remnants of Old Russia's teahouses have disappeared. These nineteenth-century establishments catered exclusively to men and were divided into two classes, one for wealthy merchants and the other for their carriage drivers, or *izvozchiki*. Merchants would stop in these gas-lanterned, sweat-perfumed taverns and consume up to twenty cups of tea in one sitting. Customarily, at the end of a journey, coachmen, who were notorious for their drunkenness, would ask their passengers, *'Na vodku?'* for some vodka money. This request eventually evolved into *'Na chay?'* ('For tea?'), which remains a polite way of asking for any tip.

The Art of Brewing Tea

The process of brewing tea is taken very seriously in Russia. Tea bags are used for convenience, but most Russians brew tea using loose black tea leaves from China, India, Sri Lanka (Ceylon), or Georgia.

Tea served Russian-style requires a small teapot, or *zavarka*, for brewing the concentrated tea, and a kettle or samovar for boiling water to dilute it. And, of course, as Fyodor Dostoyevsky writes in *Poor Folk*, the warmth and security provided by gathering around a humming samovar also requires special people.

> I would find myself remembering even the most trivial objects in the house with affection. I would think and think: how good it would be to be at home right now! I would sit in our little room, by the samovar, together with my own folk; it would be so warm, so good, so familiar. How tightly, how warmly I would embrace Mother, I would think. I would think and think, and quietly start to cry from heartbreak, choking back the tears, and forgetting all my vocabulary.

Brewing Tea, Russian-Style
[CHAYEPITIYE]

To make Russian-style tea, bring about 6 cups water to a boil. Rinse out the teapot with some of the boiling water. Put 2 teaspoons sugar and 1 level teaspoon tea leaves per person in the pot, and then add one more teaspoon of tea for the pot. Fill the teapot to capacity with boiling water, replace the lid, and cover the pot with a tea cozy or a thick dish towel. Let it steep for at least 5 minutes.

To serve, fill each cup about one-third to one-half full,

depending on the desired strength, with the tea concentrate. Then fill the cups with boiling water from the samovar or kettle. Replenish the teapot containing the tea concentrate with boiling water, cover the teapot to keep it warm, and let it sit for at least 10 minutes before the second serving.

Cabbage Pie

[PIROG S NACHINKOY IZ KAPUSTY]

A house is beautiful, not because of its walls, but because of its pies.

– Popular Russian saying

The *pirog*, or pie, is to Russians what the hamburger is to many Americans, a daily staple. It can be made from any kind of dough – yeast dough, sour cream dough, or a simple pie dough. The filling can be sweet, such as fresh apples or jam, or savory, such as meat and onion, cabbage and hard-boiled eggs, or fish with mushrooms, rice, or *kasha*.

The word *pirog* is derived from the word *pir*, which means 'feast,' and that is one prerequisite for serving a Russian pie – there should be enough people present to consume all of it.

Russians usually shape and bake their pies on baking sheets. I prefer to use a baking pan for more consistent results. As soon as the pie comes out of the oven, Russians brush the top with melted butter, and then they cover it with a clean cloth to keep it warm until serving.

Cabbage and Hard-Boiled Egg Filling

MAKES ONE 13 X 9-INCH PIE; SERVES 8 TO 10

4 tablespoons (½ stick) unsalted butter

2 tablespoons canola oil

1½ pounds cabbage, tough outer leaves and core removed, tough ribs trimmed, and cut into ¼-inch pieces

1 teaspoon salt

½ teaspoon sugar

3 hard-boiled eggs, chopped

1 recipe Yeast Dough (page 102)

To make the cabbage filling, heat the butter and oil in a large nonstick skillet over medium-high heat until the butter melts. Add the cabbage, reduce the heat to medium, and cook, stirring occasionally, for about 15 minutes, or until the cabbage is soft and most of the liquid has evaporated. Remove from the heat, add the salt and sugar, and let cool completely.

Add the hard-boiled eggs to the filling and gently mix until well combined; set aside.

To assemble and bake the pie, preheat the oven to 350 degrees F. Butter a 13 x 9 x 2-inch baking pan and set aside.

Lightly flour a work surface. Dip your hands in the flour, pick up the dough, and form it into a ball. Cut the ball in two equal parts. Using a rolling pin, roll one portion of the dough into a 14 x 10-inch rectangle. Fold it in half, transfer it to the prepared pan and unfold it. Fit the dough into the pan, and use your fingers to create an even ½-inch overhang all around. Distribute the filling evenly over the dough and set aside.

On a lightly floured work surface, roll out the remaining portion of dough into a 13 x 9-inch rectangle. Fold it in half, then carefully lift the dough, place it on top of the filling, and unfold it to cover the filling. Pinch and twist the edges of the dough together to completely seal them. Make sure that all the edges are well sealed, or the top will detach during baking. Prick the top of the dough with a fork, cover with a dish towel, and allow to rise for 10 minutes.

Bake for 30 minutes. If the top is not golden brown after 30 minutes, place the pie under the broiler for a few minutes. Let the pie cool to room temperature.

If the pie will be eaten within 4 hours, it can be left at room temperature; otherwise, it should be refrigerated, then reheated in the oven before serving. (Any leftovers should be covered and refrigerated.)

Russian-Style Apple Pie
[YABLOCHNY PIROG]

Every Russian cook has her own recipe for apple pie – by far the most popular pie in Russia. Most traditional apple pies are made with a yeast-dough crust, with the apple filling sandwiched between two layers of dough. The result is a wonderfully delicate 'apple sandwich' that is a special treat for breakfast, tea or coffee.

During late summer, fresh apples are used, as in this recipe; during the winter months, when fresh apples are scarce or prohibitively expensive, a homemade apple jam (sliced apples cooked in syrup) is substituted for the fresh apple filling. I have called for cinnamon, nutmeg, allspice, and ginger in this recipe, although none of these are traditional Russian spices.

Apple Filling
MAKES ONE 13 X 9-INCH PIE; SERVES 8 TO 10

2 pounds (about 5 large) Granny Smith, Rome, Stayman, or other firm tart cooking apples, peeled, cored, and sliced

½ cup granulated sugar

1 teaspoon ground cinnamon

Dash each of ground nutmeg, ground allspice, and powdered ginger (optional)

1 recipe Yeast Dough (page 102)

Confectioners' sugar, for dusting

To make the apple filling, combine the ingredients in a non-reactive 2-quart saucepan and cook over high heat, stirring occasionally, until the apples begin to release their juices, about 3 minutes. Reduce the heat to low and cook for 10 minutes, or until most of the liquid has evaporated and the apples are soft. Remove from the heat and let cool. (The filling can be made up to 3 days in advance, cover and refrigerate.)

To assemble and bake the pie, follow the instructions for Cabbage Pie, on page 99. Dust the cooled pie with confectioners' sugar and serve at room temperature.

Yeast Dough
[DROZHZHEVOYE TESTO]

This rich and buttery, yet light, yeast dough forms the base for two recipes: Cabbage Pie (page 98) and Russian-Style Apple Pie (page 100).

MAKES ENOUGH FOR ONE 13 X 9-INCH DOUBLE-CRUSTED PIE

One ¼-ounce package active dry yeast
¼ cup whole milk
¼ cup water
1 to 2 tablespoons sugar
½ teaspoon salt
1 large egg
8 tablespoons (1 stick) unsalted butter, melted and still warm
2½ cups all-purpose flour, or more as needed

Place the yeast in a large bowl or a large mixing bowl.

Combine the milk and ¼ cup water and heat to lukewarm (about 100 degrees F). Add the milk mixture to the yeast and gently whisk until the yeast has dissolved. Add the sugar, salt, egg, and butter and mix until well combined. Add half the flour and mix with the paddle attachment (or a wooden spoon if not using

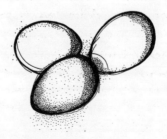

a mixer) on low speed until blended. Add the remaining flour and mix again until all the flour is well incorporated. Increase the speed to medium and continue to mix for about 5 minutes, or until the dough forms a ball. If the dough is still sticky after 3 minutes of mixing, add a little more flour, 1 tablespoon at a time, until it comes together.

Or, to knead the dough by hand, generously flour your hands and a work surface. Pick up the dough, and knead it for about 5 minutes. If it is still sticky after a few minutes of kneading, add a little more flour, 1 tablespoon at time, until the dough forms a ball. Return the dough to the bowl.

Cover the dough with plastic wrap and let rise in a warm place for about 1 hour, or until doubled in size. The dough is ready to use at this point.

Cheese Pancakes with Blueberry Sauce

[S Y R N I K I   S   C H E R N I C H N Y M   S O U S O M]

No one can turn down a bite of these cheese pancakes topped with blueberry sauce, or sauce made from any fresh or frozen berries. In Russian homes, *syrniki* are primarily served at tea (and occasionally for breakfast) with a sprinkling of sugar and a dollop of sour cream, or with fruit preserves or jam. *Syrniki*, (the name derives from the word *syr*, or cheese) are made from *tvorog*, farmer cheese. The key to making delicate *syrniki* is to use as little flour as possible. This makes the pancakes harder to flip, but the slightly creamy consistency of the finished pancakes is worth the effort.

MAKES NINE 2½-INCH PANCAKES

**8 ounces creamy farmer cheese, such as Hoop All Natural (see
Cooking Note below if you are using a less creamy brand)**
1 large egg
2 tablespoons sugar
1 teaspoon pure vanilla extract
6 tablespoons all-purpose flour
1 tablespoon raisins or dried cranberries
1 tablespoon orange marmalade or apricot jam
½ tablespoon unsalted butter, for cooking the pancakes
Blueberry Sauce (recipe follows)

Mix the farmer cheese, egg, sugar, and vanilla in a bowl until
smooth. Add the flour, raisins, and orange marmalade and continue
mixing until well blended.

Melt the butter in a large nonstick skillet over medium-high
heat. Add 1 heaping soupspoonful of the pancake batter for each
pancake and flatten slightly with the back of the spoon; do not
crowd the pancakes in the pan. Cook for 1½ to 2 minutes, or until
the bottom is golden brown. Very carefully flip each pancake and
continue cooking until golden brown on the second side, about
1½ to 2 minutes longer.

Top the pancakes with the blueberry sauce and serve
immediately.

*Cooking Note: If you are using a less creamy brand of farmer
cheese (such as Friendship All Natural Farmer Cheese), thin the
batter with 2 to 3 tablespoons milk or half-and-half.*

Blueberry Sauce

MAKES 1 CUP

½ pint fresh blueberries, washed, or 8 ounces frozen blueberries (half a 16-ounce bag), thawed and drained

⅓ cup sugar, or to taste

Combine the blueberries and sugar in a saucepan and bring to a boil, stirring occasionally, over high heat. Continue to cook until the syrup has slightly thickened, about 3 minutes. Serve warm.

A Birthday Party at Viktor's

Tatiana's Name Day, January 12th
But lo, with crimson hand
Aurora from the morning dales
leads forth, with the sun, after her
the merry name-day festival.
Since morn Dame Larin's house with guests
is filled completely; in whole families
the neighbors have converged, in winter coaches,
kibitkas, britskas, and sleighs.
— Alexander Pushkin, *Eugene Onegin*

O NE DAY, A RUSSIAN FRIEND SHOWED ME a newspaper article about Filippov's, the most famous bakery in pre-Revolutionary Moscow. This bakery supplied fresh bread by overnight train to the Czar's Winter Palace in St. Petersburg. The article mentioned the name of one of the bakers and said that his son, Viktor Novikov, was still alive in Kimry, a small town about three hours north of Moscow by car.

I wanted to meet Viktor to learn more about Filippov's, but there was no way to telephone him, and I was a little hesitant about showing up uninvited at Viktor's house. However, my Russian interpreter, Pavel, assured me that I had nothing to worry about. In the spirit of true Russian hospitality, we would be most welcome. I decided to take a chance. I packed some bananas, oranges, and Bailey's Irish Cream, precious items almost impossible to find outside Moscow at the time, and then Pavel, his brother Aleksey, and I piled into my car.

Tall, thin birch and pine trees lined the sides of the road for much of the way. While passing through a village, we stopped to ask directions and buy some flowers from one of the many stout old women standing outside their weather-beaten homes selling fresh produce from their gardens. Their small tables were overflowing with herbs, beets, potatoes, apples, raspberries, and brilliant just-picked flowers.

When we finally arrived in Kimry, we proceeded to the local police station to ask for Viktor Novikov's address. Surprisingly, without hesitation, the police gave us the number of his house located on the only street, which ran through the center of town.

Viktor's house, like most others in the neighborhood, was surrounded by a high rusty metal fence painted ocher. When he heard our car pull up, Viktor emerged to investigate. He was a small man in his late seventies with white hair, a high forehead, soft features, and a thin moustache. We got out of the car and explained that we had read about him and his father in the newspaper and had come from Moscow to meet him. Once Viktor recovered from the initial surprise of our arrival, warmth filled his soft blue-gray eyes and he invited us into his home to discuss his father's life and to join the celebration of his daughter Tatyana's fiftieth birthday that day.

Behind the creaky, rusty gates was a beautiful garden. Like a proud father showing off his children, Viktor gave us a tour, pointing out his twelve apple trees which produced over twenty varieties of apples, his pear trees, which he was grafting with black currant to increase the fruits' ability to withstand early frosts, and his prized black Minorca hens which were running loose around the yard.

We sat down at a round table surrounded by green wooden benches under a canopy of apple trees. Viktor poured vodka and began telling us about his life, about his father's work at Filippov's, and about his apple trees and hens. 'It is my dream to die in a beautiful place,' Viktor said, 'and this garden is my paradise. All I have to do is wake up in the morning, come into my garden, and I am happy.'

While we chatted, basking in the warmth of the afternoon sun, Viktor's wife and daughter prepared a feast in the kitchen. At five o'clock, they beckoned us to the table, laden with *zakuski* – fresh cucumber and tomato slices, radishes, canned sturgeon, and sliced *sosiski*, Russian salami. The toasting began – to Tatyana's birthday, to America, and to our arrival and the beginning of a long friendship.

Shchi, a hearty cabbage soup garnished with lots of fresh herbs, was brought to the table with a bowl of sour cream. Fried potatoes and roasted pork followed, as the toasts continued. 'To your health,' I raised my glass to Viktor, who responded in the customary Russian fashion by symbolically spitting over his left shoulder and knocking on wood three times.

A walnut birthday cake – without candles – was brought out, and instead of singing we toasted again. We sipped tea served from a samovar, ate cake, and then, with a sly grin, Viktor took my hand in one of his and an unopened bottle of lemon vodka in

the other, and he led me and the rest of the party back to the table in the garden, where we all shared more stories.

Viktor explained that his father left Filippov's to open a bakery in Korcheva. 'My father was loved by all the people of the town for his generosity and kindness. Frequently, poor, hungry people came into his shop to ask for free bread. My dad always gave them bread, saying as he did, If you have money, then come and pay me back; and if not, by all means, come back anyway.'

At the end of the day, as we found our way back to the car, Viktor invited us to come back the following April to celebrate his eightieth birthday, and we did. Again, the hospitality was abundant and the spirit warm. Viktor played the accordion and sang, and I sat marveling at the generosity of a man who had opened his home and his life to a complete stranger who had just stumbled across his name in a newspaper.

A Russian Baker's Story

The most famous baker in pre-Revolutionary Russia was Ivan Filippov. His establishment in Moscow not only provided the best breads in that town, but also shipped them to St. Petersburg and to the largest cities in Siberia … He himself attributed his success to the choice of ingredients … Instead of going to wholesalers, he sent his buyers directly to the mills, where they supervised the process and delivered flour that was superior to any other found on the market. Filippov also believed that Moscow water was especially beneficial for rye bread. Indeed, bread baked in St. Petersburg according to his recipes never tasted as good as his Moscow breads. As a result, he was called upon to cater a variety of breads for the court, sending them nightly to St. Petersburg by train.

– Anne Volokh, *The Art of Russian Cooking*

In Viktor Novikov's own words, here is the story of his father's life as a gifted young baker at Filippov's. Viktor became his father's apprentice, and he too pursued a career in the baking business. He does not bake anymore because he says that he can't afford the ingredients and he doesn't have the time.

My father came from a family of bakers. All his brothers and sisters were somehow connected to the baking business. In pre-Revolutionary Russia, it took two years of study to become a baker. My father was eleven years old when he came to Moscow to apprentice at Filippov's Bakery. His apprenticeship covered a range of skills from baking cakes and pies to making candies and ice cream.

When he arrived at Filippov's door, he was asked what he wanted to study and he replied, 'Everything.' The manager at Filippov's told him that it would take ten years to learn all the different skills, and therefore he should just choose one or two on which to concentrate. But my father didn't give in, and eventually his persistence awarded him the right to learn everything.

During those ten years, he was not paid. Instead, he received room and board for his work. Despite his young age, he worked diligently, neatly, and creatively. He passed all his exams with top marks in all subjects. His diploma was notarized with the Old Russian state seal.

Eventually, my father was paid well. His wages were high enough that we could afford to move into an expensive apartment close to Red Square. My mother, who worked as a seamstress at the time, could afford to wear gold jewelry. But working twelve-hour days, seven days a week, was too much for my father. He wanted to spend time with his family. He had three children. I am the youngest.

The managers at Filippov's did not agree to scale back my father's hours or those of any of the other employees, so he and the rest of the kitchen brigade went on strike. All the strikers were fired and were forced to leave Moscow within twenty-four hours. My father had a family meeting and we collectively decided to move to Korcheva, my mother's birthplace, which was also home to many rich people. My father turned to one of them for help. His name was Iponeshnikov. He owned several bakeries both in Moscow and in St. Petersburg, and he was known for his benevolence. My father presented his diploma from Filippov's, hiding the fact that he had been fired. To test my father's skill, Iponeshnikov asked him to bake some very special French cookies. The results were so good that my father was hired on the spot.

My father loved working in that bakery, and he hired me and one other young man as his apprentices. We would bake cookies, chocolate *bombes* [a molded frozen dessert with an exterior layer of ice cream or sorbet and a parfait-like center], chocolate bars, *petits fours*, *pastille* candies [small round, flat candies], cakes, pies, fruit rolls, caramels, and chocolate truffles while my mother served tea to customers from a samovar that she kept boiling all day. The only recipe I have left is my father's famous ice cream. All the rest are gone.

The Revolution broke out and Iponeshnikov, fearing persecution, fled, leaving my father to run one of his shops. My father continued the businesses and managed to feed the entire population of the town, and for this, he was loved by all the townsfolk.

I never learned how Viktor finally settled in Kimry. His father was forced to close his business, but with Lenin's New Economic Policy of the 1920s the shop was reopened, though it never reached the same level of prosperity. Viktor told us that he was working on a book about capitalism in Russia, 'to show the people how prosperous it can be.' When he is not writing, he keeps busy tending to his prized Minorca hens and his garden, and he makes his own fruit-flavored wine. Viktor's favorite dessert these days is blueberry pie topped with sour cream.

Vegetable Platter
[ZAKUSKI IZ OVOSHCHEY]

During the warmer months, when fresh produce is abundant in the markets and in the garden, a large platter of artistically arranged tomato wedges, cucumber and green pepper slices, pickles, radishes, green onions, and sprigs of cilantro and dill can be found on just about every Russian dinner table. Dinner guests tear up the herbs to sprinkle on top of their food, or they simply chomp on a whole herb sprig.

During the colder months, the fresh produce is usually replaced by homemade or market-bought pickles, salted tomatoes, salted mushrooms, or salted cabbage. Whatever the season, the salad usually remains on the table from the *zakuska* course until the dessert course. Any salty items on the platter, such as pickles or mushrooms, are used as a chaser to vodka swigs throughout the meal. No salad dressing is served, only salt.

SERVES 4

2 large ripe tomatoes, cut into wedges

1 small green bell pepper, cored, seeded, quartered, and cut into
 ¼-inch slices

2 medium cucumbers, peeled and sliced lengthwise

2 large deli-style dill pickles, sliced lengthwise

2 green onions, trimmed

A small bunch of radishes, trimmed

Sprigs of fresh dill

Sprigs of fresh cilantro

Salt

Arrange the tomatoes, pepper, cucumbers and pickles on a large platter. Garnish with the green onions, radishes, and sprigs of dill and cilantro. Pass salt at the table.

Russian Cabbage Soup
[SHCHI]

'*Shchi* and *kasha*, that's our food,' goes the old Russian saying which illustrates the popularity of cabbage soup. There are many variations of this dish, but the two most popular versions are *shchi*, made from fresh cabbage, and *kislye shchi*, made from sauerkraut or salted cabbage. Starting in the fall just before the first frost, villagers make huge quantities of salted cabbage, which they store in oak barrels. In the city, salted cabbage is usually purchased at the market, where it is sold from large plastic tubs. The discriminating shopper is invited to sample the cabbage before buying it to make sure that it has not lost its charm in the aging process.

Salted cabbage or sauerkraut versions of *shchi* are primarily consumed during the long winter months, while the fresh cabbage soup is made during the spring and summer. There is also a special, delicate *shchi* made from the very first cabbage sprouts of spring – this soup is a real celebration for Russian villagers who live off the land and cook by the seasons.

Some other types include green *shchi*, made from spinach and sorrel; nettle *shchi*, made from tender young nettles; fish *shchi*, with fish broth; mushroom *shchi*, with mushroom broth; and lazy *shchi*, made from large chunks of cabbage rather than neatly shredded or cut cabbage. Both the fish and mushroom versions are served during Lent.

No matter which kind you try, this soul-warming Russian soup is always better on the second day, after the flavors have had a chance to develop. The Russian name for this 'second-day soup' is *sutochnye shchi*, from *sutki*, the word for a twenty-four-hour period.

SERVES 6 TO 8

1½ pounds beef shank cross cuts

2 bay leaves

7 black peppercorns

Salt

2 quarts water

2 medium potatoes, peeled and cut into thin matchsticks

8 ounces white cabbage, tough outer leaves and core removed, quartered, and very thinly sliced

2 large carrots, cut into thin matchsticks

1 large ripe tomato, cut into small dice, or one 14.5-ounce can diced tomatoes, drained

2 tablespoons canola oil

1 large onion, finely diced

1 large garlic clove, minced

Salt and freshly ground pepper

3 tablespoons chopped fresh parsley

3 tablespoons chopped fresh dill

Sour cream, for serving

Combine the beef shank, bay leaves, peppercorns, 2 teaspoons salt, and water in a large pot and bring to a boil. Reduce the heat and gently simmer, uncovered, for about 1 hour, skimming as needed.

Add the potatoes, cabbage, carrots, and tomato, cover, and continue to simmer for 15 minutes.

Meanwhile, heat the canola oil in a small nonstick skillet over medium-high heat until hot. Add the onion and sauté, stirring occasionally, until dark golden brown, about 12 minutes. Add the garlic and continue to sauté for 1 minute, stirring frequently.

Add the onion and garlic, and any juices from the skillet, to the soup. Cover and simmer for 30 minutes more. Remove the soup from the heat and cool to room temperature, then refrigerate overnight.

To serve, skim any fat off the top of the soup. Reheat, adjust the seasoning, ladle into serving bowls or a soup tureen, then garnish with the parsley and dill. Pass the sour cream at the table.

A Walnut Birthday Cake
[OREKHOVY TORT]

Walnut cakes come in endless varieties in Russia. This rich cake, with a buttery, shortbread-like crust and nutty meringue topping, is the best. Serve it with tea or coffee or for dessert, topped with a dollop of whipped cream. It is even better the second day, after the topping has settled into the crust.

MAKES ONE 9-INCH CAKE; SERVES 6 TO 8

Unsalted butter and flour for greasing and flouring the cake pan

Shortbread Dough
   1½ cups all-purpose flour
   8 tablespoons (1 stick) unsalted butter, cut into pieces
   ¼ teaspoon salt
   ¼ teaspoon baking soda
   3 large egg yolks (reserve the whites for the filling)
   ½ cup granulated sugar

Walnut Filling
   2 cups chopped walnuts
   ⅓ cup dark or golden raisins
   ¼ cup lightly packed brown sugar
   3 large egg whites
   ⅛ teaspoon fresh lemon juice
   2 tablespoons granulated sugar
   4 tablespoons (½ stick) unsalted butter, melted

Confectioners' sugar, for dusting

Adjust an oven rack to the second-to-the-lowest level and pre-heat the oven to 350 degrees F. Butter a 9-inch round cake pan, dust lightly with flour, and set aside.

To make the dough, combine the flour and butter in a medium bowl. Using your fingers, in a quick rubbing motion, mix the flour and butter until the mixture resembles coarse bread crumbs. Add the salt and baking soda and continue mixing until well incorporated. Set aside.

Combine the egg yolks and sugar in a small mixing bowl and beat with an electric mixer on medium speed until light and fluffy, about 2 minutes. Add the yolk mixture to the flour mixture and mix with a wooden spoon until all of the ingredients are well blended.

Transfer the dough to the prepared cake pan. Using your hands, evenly press the dough over the bottom and up the sides of the pan, forming a neat and even 1-inch overhang about ¼ inch thick all around. Prick the bottom of the dough with a fork and refrigerate the dough-lined pan while you make the filling.

To make the filling, combine the walnuts, raisins, and brown sugar in a medium bowl and mix until well blended. Set aside.

Combine the egg whites and lemon juice in the large bowl of an electric mixer and beat on low speed for 30 seconds. Increase the speed to medium and beat for about 30 seconds, or until foamy. Add the granulated sugar and beat for 30 seconds more. Increase the speed to high and beat for about 1 minute, or until stiff peaks form.

Using a rubber spatula, gently fold the egg whites into the walnut mixture until just combined, then fold in the melted butter. Distribute the walnut filling evenly in the dough-lined pan and bake for 35 to 40 minutes, or until the crust and meringue top are golden brown and a knife inserted in the center comes out clean. Check the cake after 20 minutes; if the top is browning too fast, place a piece of foil loosely over it. Allow the cake to cool completely, then invert it upside down onto a plate and, using another plate, flip it over so it is upright. Serve the cake at room temperature. (Leftovers should be covered and stored at room temperature.)

Russian Summers: A Time for Preserving the Bounty

The best season, of course, is summer, because we have fresh produce from our garden. You know, you walk into the garden and pick up a large red beet and here is your dinner – both soup and main course. I also make *okroshka* [a *kvas*-based fresh vegetable soup served chilled] with cucumbers, radishes, parsley, and dill – all from my garden . . . We make lots of cabbage salads, radish salads, and garden salads. We eat noodles with sautéed mushrooms we gather from the forest, and we eat potatoes just pulled from the ground.

– Mariya, a year-round inhabitant of the village of Kosilova

RUSSIAN SUMMERS ARE SHORT, HOT, AND BUSY, particularly for Russian villagers. The days are long, especially during the 'White Nights' of June, and the daylight hours are reserved solely for work. Houses must be maintained, roofs repaired, gardens planted and harvested, wood chopped and stacked, and, most important, summer's bounty must be stored.

Preserving and pickling in summer are the keys to survival in winter. Nature's timetable is strictly followed: strawberries and apricots in June, raspberries and black cherries in July, currants and plums in August. Salting cucumbers and tomatoes begins in mid-June and goes on all summer long; pickling starts only at the end of summer, with cabbage the last to be done. In addition, root vegetables are buried in sand, covered layer by layer with straw. Fruits are wrapped in paper and packed into wooden barrels, again in layers separated by straw.

From the outside, Mariya's *dacha*, like all others in the village of Kosilova, looks like a brightly painted gingerbread house; white wooden lace fringes the eaves and windows. A wooden fence with painted finials surrounds each house, and on the road side of the fence is a bench where passers-by can sit down for a long gossip.

Mariya is dressed like most of the other village women. Her worn and stained working clothes are covered by a large apron, a kerchief is tied to keep her hair back, and on her feet are boots, mud-caked or clean depending on the weather. The fresh country air has kept her face almost wrinkle-free, but her hands show the wear and tear of someone who lives off the land. Mariya's deep blue eyes and warm smile reflect her cheerful, optimistic personality. She moves with purpose to complete her many daily chores and to care for her aging father. But Mariya does not complain. She and the other year-round inhabitants of Kosilova have learned to accept nature and life as they are – beautiful and less-than-perfect.

Inside, Mariya's *dacha* is a simple log cabin with no running water. A painted-white brick *pech*, or traditional Russian stove, standing five feet high, takes up a third of the main room. The *pech* is so central to Russian country life that people used to kiss it goodbye and ask for its blessing and protection before leaving on a long journey. Indeed, the *pech* serves to provide all the necessities of Russian life: to heat the house, to dry snow-soaked clothes or laundry in the winter, to heat the iron, to bake *pirogi* (pies), to simmer soups and stews, and to boil water for tea. No longer do people sleep on it, though, as was the custom in the past.

An oil lamp, kept lit day and night, hangs suspended over the *krasny ugol*, or sacred corner, where an icon stands in an intricately carved wooden holder draped with colorful embroidered cloths.

Red plastic flowers are tucked into the frame of the icon itself. But at this time of year, the *krasny ugol* has to vie for attention, visually if not spiritually, with all the produce Mariya has gathered to store and preserve: apples, potatoes, carrots, beets, cabbage, cucumbers, tomatoes, mushrooms, and herbs.

In the room next to the kitchen, onion and garlic braids hang down from hooks, and jars of fruit preserves line the shelves. Burlap sacks of dried corn for the chickens lean against the cupboard. Huge wicker baskets and wooden crates filled to over-flowing with yellow and red apples sit on the bed waiting to be dried or salted or made into jam. Over the bed hang two home-made fishing rods for catching pike in the nearby lake.

When Mariya gave up keeping farm animals, the old stable behind the house was made over, half as a coop for the chickens and half as a pantry. Birch branches hang from the rafters, drying to become brushes for use in the *banya*, or Russian bath, akin to a dry sauna. In the *banya*, people beat each other with birch branches in the belief that it opens the pores and improves circulation. The sauna is often followed by a jump in the river or lake or, in winter, a roll in the snow.

The dirt floor of Mariya's pantry is thickly covered with straw for insulation, and the pantry is stocked with five-liter green-tinted *banki* (jars) of pickled cucumbers and tomatoes and smaller jars of strawberry, raspberry, and black currant preserves. Buckets of salted mushrooms covered only with plates and dish towels – Mariya never puts her salted mushrooms in lidded jars – stand in the corner. Potatoes are stored under the floorboards near the stove in the house.

Even with the new space made for the pantry in the old stable, there is never enough room in autumn for all the food. More buckets of salted mushrooms and apples are stored in the entry, next to muddy boots and below the heavy fleece-lined coat that Mariya will put on when winter comes.

The Art of Making Fruit Preserves

For city dwellers, summer carries with it the promise of weekend escapes to the *dacha*. In many families, it is customary for the women and children to relocate to the countryside for the entire season. They escape the city's heat, smog, and *pukh* (translated as 'down' in Russian and referring to the 'summer snow' produced by the balsam poplar in June). This tree, abundant in Moscow and a curse to anyone with allergies, releases seeds coated with white cottony fluff, creating a blizzard-like effect at times, complete with 'snow drifts' in street gutters and on sidewalks. Some Muscovites blame Stalin for this fluff, while others blame Nikita Khrushchev for planting masses of these fast-growing female trees to add quick greenery to Moscow's streets.

Whether in the city or at the country *dacha*, as fruit comes into season, Russians always set aside time to preserve some of it. Apart from being an essential part of the tea service, fruit preserves are believed to cure everything from the common cold to constipation and poor eyesight. Any vitamins they provide are an added bonus.

I was taught how to make *varenye* by Antonina, the friend who hosted our memorable tea party in Strogino (page 87). Her methods are simple, and her *varenye* are exquisite. 'When you try my *varenye*,' she told me proudly, 'you don't feel the sugar in your mouth, only the berries.' In Antonina's preserves, each piece of fruit holds its shape perfectly in thick translucent syrup. She stores the preserves in jars under her couch for two years or more. 'Like good wine, they improve with age,' she says.

Part of the secret of making successful *varenye* is selecting the right fruit. It should be uniform in size, undamaged, and, usually, not completely ripe. Berries should be preserved the day they are picked or bought, preferably after several days of dry weather, because rainwater-logged berries tend to lose their shape and flavor when preserved.

For the same reason, Antonina spreads out her berries on several thicknesses of newspaper to drain after she washes them. (Raspberries are not washed.) Draining the berries on newspapers also cuts down on stains, which can be a real problem, especially with black or blue bilberries, a cousin of the North American blueberry.

Russian preserves are put up in green-tinted glass jars that are hermetically sealed with a kind of wrench-like device. Some Russians still follow the old practice of sealing the jars with a piece of paper or cloth soaked in vodka or brandy (Antonina sprinkles vodka over the berries instead), but paraffin is never used. Nor are the preserves traditionally processed in a hot-water bath. (Note: If you prepare any of these recipes, it is imperative that you observe common-sense measures and process your preserves to avoid any possibility of food poisoning. Precise instructions are given below.)

Before reliable canning jars and refrigeration were available, Russians sugared their preserves heavily and then boiled them for a long time. Nowadays, they are less sweet – though still very sweet to the Western palate – and more delicate. In the method taught to me by Antonina, certain fruits, such as raspberries and strawberries, are sprinkled with vodka, covered with sugar, and left to macerate overnight. The next day, as the preserves are brought to a boil, the foam is removed several times. In typically frugal fashion, Russians save this foam to eat with tea, just as cherry, peach, and other fruit pits are saved to flavor vodka. The foam is surprisingly good; it resembles Jolly Rancher hard candies. Any leftover syrup is combined with water to make *sok*, a refreshing and nutritious fruit drink.

Techniques for making *varenye* vary from person to person and from fruit to fruit. For example, Antonina boils her strawberry *varenye* only once, but others, like my friend Natalya, boil the strawberries in sugar syrup several times, letting the mixture rest in between. Both women use the resting-period method for apricot *varenye*. A third method, the so-called five-minute preserving technique, is used for some fruits; it is particularly well suited to the bilberry.

Russians also make *dzhem*, or Western-style jam, which is used for cake and pie filling but rarely spread on bread – though it is delicious that way. *Vitamin*, an uncooked mixture of fruit, usually strawberries, raspberries, red currants, or *feioja* (also known as pineapple guava), and sugar, is eaten the same way as *varenye*. To make *vitamin*, the fruit and sugar are combined in a bowl and whisked until the sugar has completely dissolved and the mixture resembles a thick purée.

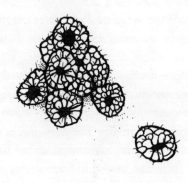

Lightly Salted Cucumbers

[SOLYONYE OGURTSY]

> Whereupon the host and his guest went up to the table which was laid with snacks and, as is the custom, drank a glass of vodka each and had some snacks as is done throughout the whole length and breadth of Russia, in the towns as well as the villages, that is to say, they tasted all sorts of salt pickles and other stimulating delicacies and then proceeded to the dining-room, the mistress of the house walking in front of them like a staid goose.
>
> – Nikolay Gogol, *Dead Souls*

Even though lightly salted cucumbers are available from the barrel in their local markets, most Russians make their own all summer long. These cucumbers are the traditional companion to vodka, and can be found on most vegetable *zakuska* platters. As soon as the last words of a toast are uttered, a Russian picks up a salted cucumber or pickle with one hand and a glass of vodka

with the other. He inhales deeply and exhales, then, with a pensive look, raises the glass to his lips, closes his eyes, tilts his head back, and swallows the contents in one gulp. Quickly, he takes a bite of pickle to overcome the burn of the spirits. A glass of pickle brine is a popular remedy for a vodka hangover, a vicious reminder of yesterday's overindulgence.

Cold fermentation with salt is by far the most popular way to salt cucumbers, though the vinegar-with-heat method is also used, mainly for long-term preservation. Years ago, cucumbers were pickled in oak barrels, which now have been replaced by 10-liter *banki*, or jars. This recipe is for a smaller amount, two quarts.

Sour cherry leaves are believed to keep the cucumbers firm; black currant and horseradish leaves are added for their reputed medicinal qualities. Sea salt is preferred for pickling because it is free of additives, which might cloud the brine. That is also the reason for using spring water. Bouquets of these leaves are sold in small bundles in the markets during the pickling season. Unfortunately, these leaves are hard to find in the United States; but I have included the recipe anyway, to show you the traditional method of lightly salting cucumbers.

Cooking Note: Standing time 4 days

MAKES 2 QUARTS

2¼ pounds small cucumbers (about 14), such as Kirbys or other pickling cucumbers, each about 3½ inches long and 1¼ inches thick

1 small unblemished fresh horseradish leaf, washed and cut into 6 or more pieces

2 unblemished fresh black currant leaves, washed

6 unblemished fresh sour cherry leaves, washed

2 stems fresh dill with yellow flowers, washed

2 small garlic cloves, halved

4⅓ cups spring water or bottled water
2 tablespoons sea salt

Sterilize 2 wide-mouthed quart canning jars as directed on pages 130-131. Leave them in hot water or in the oven until ready to use.

Wash the cucumbers well, removing any stems. Trim a very thin slice from each end to expose the flesh. Place the cucumbers in a bowl of ice water and set aside.

Line the bottom and sides of each jar with some of each kind of leaf, setting aside a leaf or piece of leaf for the top. Divide the dill and garlic between the jars. Drain the cucumbers and arrange them standing up in the jars, packing them tightly together but allowing the leaves, dill, and garlic to come between some of them.

Bring the water to a boil. Remove from the heat and add the salt, stirring until the salt dissolves. Pour the hot brine into the jars, filling them to within ⅜-inch of the top. Make sure the cucumbers are fully submerged, weighing them down if necessary with a sterilized heatproof cup or mug. Cover with a single layer of cheese-cloth and set aside in a cool place (60 to 65 degrees F) for 48 hours.

Sterilize the jar lids. Remove the cheesecloth and seal the jars with the lids. Refrigerate for 2 days before eating. Once opened, the cucumbers will keep for about 2 weeks in the refrigerator.

Cooking Note: Don't be alarmed if the brine turns cloudy at the bottom after the cucumbers have been in it for a day or two; this is natural. It is also natural for the garlic to turn blue.

Food Safety and Handling
for Preserves and Jam

Varenye and *dzhem* can be put up in quart- or pint-sized (liter- or half-liter-sized) jars; for *varenye*, in particular, the jars should be wide-mouthed so you can get the fruit in without damaging it. The following procedures, for Mason jars with a two-part lid, are recommended for safe canning.

Sterilizing the Jars: If you are reusing jars, check them and reject any with cracks, chips, or sharp edges. Always use new lids. Wash the jars, lids, and bands in soapy water and rinse, or run them through the dishwasher. The jars should be hot when filled. To keep the jars hot, do one of the following:

1. Put the jars in a large pot, cover with water, and bring to a boil. Reduce the heat and simmer (at 180 degrees F) for 15 minutes. Turn off the heat and leave the jars in the water until ready to use. Just before filling, invert onto a folded dish towel to dry. Or,

2. Place the jars on a baking sheet and keep in a low oven (250 degrees F) for 20 minutes before filling.

Sterilizing the Lids: Place the lids and bands in a small bowl or pan and pour boiling water over them to soften the rubber seals for 3 to 5 minutes.

Filling the Jars: Fill the hot jars with hot preserves only to within ⅜ inch of the top, to allow for headroom. Wipe the rims with a damp cloth and seal with a hot lid. Screw on the metal band as tightly as you can, or as the manufacturer directs. Invert the jar for 5 minutes after filling, then proceed with a hot-water bath.

Hot-water Bath: Place the filled and sealed jars on a rack or on a folded cloth in a canning kettle or deep pot. They should not touch each other or the sides of the pot. Cover with at least 1 inch of water, cover the pot, bring to a boil, and boil for 15 to 20 minutes. Remove the jars with tongs and let stand, away from drafts, until completely cool. Do not retighten the bands. After 12 to 24 hours, test the seal by pressing the center of each lid. If it stays down, the seal is good. If not, store the jar in the refrigerator.

Labeling and Storing the Preserves: Always label jars with the contents and date. Preserves stored in a cool, dark, dry place will retain their color, flavor, and food value for at least a year.

Serving: Always use a clean spoon to remove the *varenye* or *dzhem* (or any other jelly or jam) from the jar.

Strawberry Preserves

[KLUBNICHNOYE VARENYE]

Contemporary Muscovites, constrained by their small kitchens and lack of storage space, make *varenye* in quantities similar to those in the accompanying recipes. Many still use the old-fashioned wide copper pan with sloping sides that gives the *varenye* plenty of room to foam up. Traditionally these pans have a very long wooden handle. When the preserves were made over an open fire, the pan rested on a tripod, and the long handle made it easy to remove it and to swirl the contents and collect the foam.

In the nineteenth-century Russian countryside, *varenye* was made in huge quantities, as described in the following scene from Gogol's short story, *Old-World Landowners:*

[Pulkheria Ivanovna's] house was very much like a chemical laboratory. There was always a fire built under an apple tree; and cauldron or a copper pan of jam, jelly, or fruit cheese made with honey, sugar, and I don't remember what else, was scarcely ever taken off the iron tripod on which it stood. Under another tree the coachman was forever distilling in a copper retort [a closed laboratory vessel with an outlet tube used for distillation by heat] vodka with peach leaves, or bird-cherry flowers or centaury [a plant similar to the cornflower] or cherry stones, and at the end of the process was utterly unable to control his tongue, jabbered such nonsense that Pulkheria Ivanovna could make nothing of it, and had to go away to sleep it off in the kitchen.

In Russia, Victoria strawberries, which ripen early in June, are used to make these preserves. They are small, dark red, and very meaty. With a ratio of four parts sugar to five parts fruit by weight, the preserves are quite sweet.

Cooking Note: Standing time overnight, or up to 15 hours.

MAKES ABOUT 4 PINTS

3½ pounds small firm, juicy strawberries just at the peak of
   ripeness
2 tablespoons vodka (optional)
3 pounds sugar (about 6¾ cups)

Rinse the strawberries well under cold running water and spread out on paper towels or newspapers to drain. Carefully hull the berries, without cutting deeply into the flesh and place them in a large bowl. Sprinkle the berries with the vodka if using, and cover evenly with the sugar, leaving no berries exposed to the air if possible. Cover the bowl with a dish towel and let stand at room temperature overnight, or for up to 15 hours.

Transfer the berries, sugar, and all the accumulated juices to a 5-quart heavy nonreactive pot and bring to a boil. Reduce the heat and simmer for 25 to 35 minutes without stirring (possibly quite a bit longer). Every 5 minutes or so, lift the pan and gently swirl the contents, to collect the foam in the center. Remove the foam with a spoon and return the pan to the heat. The berries have cooked long enough when they have lost their bright color and turned a subdued red, like strawberries baked in a pie. They should be plump and suspended in syrup. To test, place a drop of syrup on a plate; it should hold its bubble-like shape and not run. If it does run, continue to simmer and check for doneness at 10-minute intervals.

While the preserves are cooking, sterilize 4 wide-mouthed pint jar and lids as described on pages 130-131.

When the preserves are ready, fill the hot jars to capacity, leaving ⅜-inch of headroom. Take care to keep the berries intact. Wipe the jar rims clean with a damp cloth, seal the jars, and flip them over for five minutes. If you have any preserves left over, ladle them into a clean small jar and refrigerate.

Process the jars in a hot-water bath as described on pages 130-131 for 15 to 20 minutes. Remove the jars from the water bath and let cool to room temperature.

Store the jars in a cool dark place; they will keep well for at least 1 year. Once a jar has been opened, store it in the refrigerator for up to 1 month.

Apricot Preserves
[ABRIKOSOVOYE VARENYE]

In Russia, the almond-like apricot seeds, or kernels, contained in the pits are added to the fruit at the end of the cooking process. I have omitted this step because the apricot kernels contain trace amounts of cyanide.

Cooking Note: Standing time 2 days

MAKES ABOUT 4 PINTS

4½ pounds very small firm, undamaged, and slightly underripe apricots

3½ pounds sugar (about 7 ½ cups)

Remove any stems and leaves from the apricots. Wash and drain them. Following the natural seam, cut each apricot almost in half, leaving a section of flesh uncut so that the two halves are still attached. Carefully remove the pits and discard.

Place the apricots in a large bowl and cover evenly with the sugar, leaving no apricots exposed to the air if possible. Cover the bowl with a dish towel and let stand at room temperature overnight, or for up to 15 hours.

First boil: After the overnight rest, transfer the apricots, sugar, and all the accumulated juices to a large pot and slowly bring to a boil. Cook over high heat for 3 minutes, without stirring. If the foam seems to be about to overflow, pick up the pot and gently swirl the contents to collect the foam in the center. Remove the foam with a spoon and return the pot to the heat. When the 5 minutes are up, remove the pot from the heat and carefully remove any foam. Cover the pot with a clean towel and let stand at room temperature for no less than 12 hours.

Second boil: After the 12-hour rest, return the pot to the heat and bring to a boil. Do not stir. Cook over high heat for 5 minutes, remove from the heat, and carefully remove any foam. Cover with a clean towel and let stand at room temperature for another 12 hours.

Third boil: Return the pot to the heat and bring to a boil. Reduce the heat and simmer, uncovered, removing foam as necessary, for 20 minutes, or until there is almost no foam left and the fruit is suspended in the syrup. To test for doneness, place a drop of syrup on a plate; it should hold its bubble-like shape and not run. If it does run, continue to simmer and check for doneness at 10-minute intervals.

Meanwhile, sterilize 4 wide-mouthed pint jars and lids as described on pages 130-131.

When the preserves are ready, fill the jars and process as directed in the recipe for Strawberry Preserves (page 133).

Jams

Russians use Western-style jams, called *dzhem*, to fill yeast-dough pies or to top pancakes. They traditionally do not use packaged or natural fruit pectin to thicken their jams. The fruit is slowly boiled down with sugar until very thick but still spreadable. Although Russians don't spread their jams on bread or toast, they are heavenly eaten that way. As with all preserves, starting with undamaged fruit at or near its peak of flavor gives best results. Russians like their jams sweet, and these recipes reflect that preference.

Strawberry Jam

[KLUBNICHNY DZHEM]

MAKES ABOUT 2½ PINTS

3 pounds very small firm, well-formed strawberries just at their peak of ripeness

2 pounds sugar (about 4½ cups)

Rinse the strawberries well under cold running water and spread out on paper towels or newspapers to drain.

Hull the berries and place them in a large heavy-bottomed non-reactive 5-quart saucepan. Using a potato masher, or your hands, crush the berries into large chunks. Add the sugar, mix well, and bring to a boil. Reduce the heat and gently simmer, uncovered, for 1 to 1½ hours, or until the syrup has thickened to a loose jam consistency. Skim the foam from the surface as needed and, using a pastry brush dipped in water, wash down the sides of the pot. During the last 30 minutes of cooking time, stir every 5 minutes to prevent scorching.

While the jam is cooking, sterilize 2 pint or 4 half-pint jars and lids as described on pages 130-131.

When the jam is ready, fill the hot jars to capacity, leaving ⅜-inch of headroom. Wipe the jar rims clean with a damp cloth, seal the jars, and flip them over for five minutes. If you have any jam left over, ladle it into a clean small jar and refrigerate.

Process the jars in a hot-water bath as described on pages 130-131 for 15 to 20 minutes. Remove the jars from the water bath and let cool to room temperature.

Store the jars in a cool, dark place; they will keep for at least 1 year. Once a jar has been opened, store it in the refrigerator for up to 1 month.

Variation

Raspberry Jam: Substitute firm well-formed dry raspberries just at their peak of ripeness for the strawberries. Do not rinse the raspberries. Cook as for Strawberry Jam, simmering the jam for about 1 hour to 1¼ hours, or until the syrup has thickened to a loose jam consistency. Fill, seal, process, and store as for Strawberry Jam.

Apricot Jam

[ABRIKOSOVY DZHEM]

Since apricots give off less juice than berries, the cooking time for apricot jam is slightly less than for berry-based jams. Russians do not add the seeds from the apricot stones to jam as they do to apricot *varenye*.

Cooking Note: Standing time overnight, or up to 15 hours.

MAKES ABOUT 2 PINTS

3 pounds firm, undamaged, slightly underripe very small apricots
2¼ pounds sugar (about 5 cups)

Remove any stems and leaves from the apricots. Wash and drain them. Following the natural seam, cut each apricot in half. Remove and discard the pits. Place the fruit in a large bowl and cover evenly with sugar, leaving no fruit exposed to the air if possible. Cover the bowl with a dish towel and let stand at room temperature overnight, or for up to 15 hours.

Transfer the fruit, sugar, and all the accumulated juices to a 5-quart heavy nonreactive pot and bring to a boil. Reduce the heat and gently simmer, uncovered, for 1 to 1¼ hours, or until the syrup has thickened to a loose jam consistency. Skim the foam from the surface as needed and, using a pastry brush dipped in water, wash down the sides of the pot. During the last 30 minutes of cooking time, stir the jam every 5 minutes to prevent scorching. As you stir the jam, crush the apricots against the sides of the pan.

While the jam is cooking, sterilize 2 pint jars or 4 half-pint jars and lids as described on pages 130-131.

When the jam is ready, fill the hot jars to capacity, leaving ⅜-inch of headroom. Wipe the jar rims clean with a damp cloth, seal the jars, and flip them over for five minutes. If you have any jam left over, ladle it into a clean small jar and refrigerate.

Process the jars in a hot-water bath as described on pages 130-131 for 15 to 20 minutes. Remove the jars from the water bath and let cool to room temperature.

Store the jars in a cool, dark place; they will keep for at least 1 year. Once a jar has been opened, store it in the refrigerator for up to 1 month.

Autumn and
Mushroom Hunting

When Autumn has just come, there is
most brief a lull: brief but divine.
All day 'tis like some precious prism,
and limpidly the evenings shine.

Where lusty sickles swung and corn-ears bent
the plain is empty now: wider it seems.
Alone a silky filament
across the idle furrow gleams.

The airy void, now birdless, is revealed,
but still remote is the first whirl of snow;
and stainless skies in mellow blueness flow
upon the hushed reposing field.
– Mikhail Lermontov, 'Autumn'

AS SUMMER'S HEAT GIVES WAY TO AUTUMN'S CRISP AIR, days grow shorter, and leaves change color, Russians grab their wicker baskets and head to the forest. For Russians, mushroom hunting is a ritual that gently eases the body and soul into the calendar's colder months.

Gathering, sorting, and preserving mushrooms – the so-called third hunt, following the first hunt, for big game, and the second for small game – is almost a mystical experience, and mushroom hunters, while proud to show off their finds, are very secretive about where they discovered them. In his autobiography, *Speak, Memory*, Vladimir Nabokov describes his mother's favorite pastime of picking mushrooms.

> One of her greatest pleasures in summer was the very Russian sport of *hodit' po gribi* (looking for mushrooms). Fried in butter and thickened with sour cream, her delicious finds appeared regularly on the dinner table. Not that the gustatory moment mattered much. Her main delight was in the quest, and this quest had its rules . . .
>
> Rainy weather would bring out these beautiful plants in profusion under the firs, birches, and aspens in our park, especially in its older part, east of the carriage road that divided the park in two. Its shady recesses would then harbor that special boletic reek which makes a Russian's nostrils dilate – a dark, dank, satisfying blend of damp moss, rich earth, rotting leaves. But one had to poke and peer for a goodish while among the wet underwood before something really nice, such as a family of bonneted baby *edulis* or the marbled variety of *scaber*, could be discovered and carefully teased out of the soil.

At sundown one Friday, four of us – Pavel, his brother Aleksey, his uncle Leonid, and I – drove out of Moscow in my red Zhiguli, a small Russian car. Heading for Kosilova, a tiny village about two hundred miles north of Moscow, we soon joined the weekend exodus of Muscovites to their *dachas*, those little huts and plots of land in the country that sustain them, body and soul. Because of our foreign license plate, we were stopped often by the *GAI*, the State Motor Vehicle Inspectorate.

'Where are you going?'

'To Kosilova, to pick mushrooms.'

With such a quintessentially Russian mission, we were waved on.

We reached Kosilova well after dark under a sky alive with stars. Yevgeny, Pavel's father, had arrived a day earlier. He welcomed us into his rebuilt *dacha*, his childhood home, which had been burned to the ground by German soldiers during World War II. We were quickly warmed by a wood fire and the earthy aroma of simmering mushrooms, which Yevgeny was getting ready to salt and jar. For dinner, he prepared a feast of sautéed wild mushrooms he had gathered that morning in the woods and boiled potatoes from his garden.

The next morning, soon after daybreak, wicker baskets on our arms, we set out on our own quest for mushrooms. The weather was perfect, sunny with a slight chill in the air and damp from the 'mushroom rains,' showers interspersed with sunshine, the day before. With Yevgeny as our guide, we found a hidden island of moss carpeted with mushrooms, hundreds and hundreds of them. We lined our baskets with ferns and filled them in no time.

Yevgeny's instructions on how to distinguish *poganki*, or poisonous mushrooms, were to the point: 'If you can't identify the mushroom by its cap,' he said, 'cut it and lick the stem. If it tastes sour, it's probably poisonous.' Never eat, or even taste a mushroom you are unsure of. Unless you are experienced in identifying which mushrooms are safe to pick and eat and which, fatally, are not, it is best to follow the adage, 'When in doubt, leave it out.' It is also advisable to consult a reputable field guide to mushrooms.

Back at the *dacha* we cleaned and sorted our mushrooms. We boiled some for canning, spread others on trays lined with fresh birch twigs to dry near the stove, and set the rest aside for dinner. In addition to chanterelles, we had found several varieties of *boletus* mushrooms (also known as porcini or cèpes), including what the Russians call 'under birches,' or brown and white birch *boletus (Leccinum scabrum and L. holopos)*, and 'under aspens,' or white poplar *boletus (L. duriusculum)*, as well as some slippery jacks *(Suillus luteus)*. We sautéed them with butter, garnished them with parsley and dill from the garden, and ate them with noodles.

The next day, we all went to visit Yevgeny's lifelong neighbors, Mariya and her father, Petr, ninety-five years old but still vigorous and unbowed by age. Mariya, wearing a soiled apron covering the many layers of clothing she puts on in true peasant fashion, was in the midst of putting up fruits and vegetables from her garden and from the woods. Sorting mushrooms as she sipped tea with us, she apologized for working while visiting. 'My hands must never be idle during the summer,' she said. 'In winter they can rest, when all the work is over.'

Sunday afternoon we drove back to the city with thousands of other Muscovites in their rickety cars, now sagging under the sacks of potatoes on the roof, the fruits and vegetables piled high on the back seat. Boxes of farm-fresh eggs and bunches of cut flowers lay on the back window ledges. The bounty of the land was going home to the city. Soon, in tiny apartments in faceless high-rises, the people of Moscow would be pickling and preserving, no less than Mariya and the other villagers of Kosilova.

Dried Mushrooms
[SUSHONYE GRIBY]

Drying mushrooms, especially *byelye griby*, or *boletus edulis* (the same as porcini or cèpes), enhances their natural fragrance. In the Russian countryside, the mushrooms are spread out on trays lined with green birch twigs or threaded onto strings like a necklace and then placed near a wood-burning stove. As the mushrooms dry, they pick up the perfume of the wood.

You can dry mushrooms, store-bought or foraged (consult a reputable field guide for safe varieties), in the oven. They won't have the unique flavor of those dried by the heat of burning wood, but they will be quite wonderful – and a lot cheaper than those sold in little cellophane bags.

To dry mushrooms, turn the oven on to as low a temperature as possible, around 200 degrees F. Place a grill – a cake rack works well – on a baking sheet. Trim and wipe the mushrooms clean, and spread them about ¼ inch apart on the grill. Leave in the oven for 15 to 24 hours, or until completely dry. Store in an airtight container or in a cloth bag. Use in Mushroom Soup (page 145) or in other recipes.

Marinated Mushrooms

[MARINOVANNYE GRIBY]

Following is a recipe for marinated mushrooms, but first a few words about Russian salted mushrooms. Salted mushrooms are used for stews, soups, and salads, but their prime purpose is for downing with a shot of vodka. The best Russian varieties for salting are so-called 'under birches' *(Leccinum scabrum and L. holopos)*, 'under aspens' *(L. duriusculum)*, and slippery jacks *(Suillus luteus)*. Salted mushrooms, with or without vodka, are very much an acquired taste, if you can get past their slimy texture.

Marinated mushrooms, on the other hand, are tasty nibbles that enhance just about any hors d'oeuvre or *zakuska* platter. Be sure to use small, young button mushrooms with tightly closed caps. This mushroom is called *shampinyon* in the Russian market, from the French *champignon*.

Cooking Note: Standing time at least 5 days.

MAKES ABOUT 1 QUART

1½ pounds firm small button mushrooms, cleaned and stems trimmed close to the caps

1 tablespoon plus 1 teaspoon noniodized salt

1 cup water

½ cup 5% white wine vinegar

3 whole cloves

2 small bay leaves

5 black peppercorns

3 whole allspice berries

1 teaspoon sugar

1 medium garlic clove, slivered

1 tablespoon oil

Sterilize a wide-mouthed 1-quart canning jar and lid (page 130).

Bring 1 quart water to a boil in a medium saucepan, add the mushrooms and 1 teaspoon of the salt, and return to a boil. Reduce the heat and simmer for 3 minutes. Drain and set aside to cool to room temperature.

Combine the 1 cup water, the vinegar, cloves, bay leaves, peppercorns, allspice, sugar, and the remaining 1 tablespoon salt in a small nonreactive saucepan. Bring to a boil, immediately remove from the heat, and skim any foam. Add the garlic and let cool to room temperature.

Spoon the mushrooms into the jar, add the marinade, and carefully pour the oil on top to form a seal. Cover tightly and refrigerate for 5 days before eating. Once opened, the mushrooms will keep for 3 to 4 weeks in the refrigerator.

Mushroom Soup

[GRIBNOY SUP]

Flowers, love, the country, idleness,
ye fields! My soul is vowed to you.
– Alexander Pushkin, *Eugene Onegin*

Russians are especially fond of this soup because it conjures up glorious days of mushroom hunting in the forests. Toward the end of the summer, the open-air markets in Moscow are lined with peddlers selling their hand-picked mushrooms. They spread their fresh porcini, chanterelles, and various other samples on newspapers lined with ferns. Dried porcini, threaded onto a string to form a wonderfully fragrant necklace, are also offered to be bought and saved for the winter months.

Fresh porcini mushrooms, or cèpes, called *byelye* in Russian, are excellent for this soup. If they are not available, substitute any other fragrant fresh or dried mushrooms, such as shiitakes. I have called for both fresh and dried mushrooms in this recipe – the fresh for their meaty texture, and the dried for the intense mushroom flavor they bring to the soup. If your dried mushrooms are not high-quality, or are a bit rubbery, you may want to add only the dried mushroom broth, not the reconstituted mushrooms.

The Russians never add stock to this soup because they claim it detracts from the intense mushroom flavor. I like to add two bouillon cubes. Flour or starch is sometimes added to thicken the soup, but rice or small pasta, such as orzo or ditalini, is my preferred thickener.

SERVES 6 TO 8

½ to 1 ounce dried mushrooms, preferably porcini

2 cups boiling water

2 tablespoons unsalted butter

1 tablespoon canola oil

1 medium onion, quartered and cut crosswise into thin slices

1 small garlic clove, minced

6 ounces fresh cremini, shiitake, or porcini mushrooms, cleaned, trimmed, and thinly sliced

1 medium potato, cut into thin matchsticks

2 large carrots, cut into thin matchsticks

⅓ cup small pasta (optional)

1½ quarts water

2 bouillon cubes (optional)

Salt and freshly ground pepper

2 tablespoons chopped fresh dill

2 tablespoons chopped fresh parsley

Sour cream, for serving

To reconstitute the dried mushrooms, place them in a bowl or heatproof measuring cup, add the boiling water, and let sit for at least 30 minutes.

Line a small sieve with a wet paper towel, set it over a bowl, and drain the mushrooms through the sieve. Save the liquid, and rinse the mushrooms thoroughly under cool running water to remove any sand or grit. Slice the mushrooms and set aside.

Heat the butter and oil in a large saucepan over medium-high heat. Add the onions and sauté until golden brown, about 7 minutes. Add the garlic and fresh mushrooms and continue to sauté for 2 minutes, or until fragrant.

Add the potato, carrots, pasta, the water, reserved mushroom liquid and reconstituted mushrooms, and bouillon cubes, if using, and bring to a boil. Reduce the heat and simmer for 15 minutes, or until the vegetables are tender.

If serving immediately, adjust the seasoning, and add the dill and parsley to the soup. Pass the sour cream at the table for guests to help themselves. If serving later, allow the soup to cool to room temperature, cover, and refrigerate. (The soup can be prepared up to 2 days in advance, cover and refrigerate.)

Potato Casserole with Mushroom Sauce

[KARTOFELNAYA ZAPEKANKA S GRIBNYM SOUSOM]

Potato *zapekanka* is a perfect side dish for just about any type of meat, poultry, or fish. It is a combination of pureed potatoes, eggs, and fresh herbs, which is baked. If I'm not serving the mushroom sauce, I like to add sautéed fresh mushrooms to the purée along with the herbs.

SERVES 4

Unsalted butter, for greasing the baking dish

Potato *Zapekanka*
1½ pounds Yukon Gold potatoes (about 6 medium), peeled
1 cup whole milk, warmed
4 tablespoons (½ stick) unsalted butter, melted
2 large eggs
1 tablespoon chopped fresh dill
1 tablespoon chopped fresh parsley
Salt and freshly ground pepper

Mushroom Sauce

MAKES ABOUT 2½ CUPS

3 ounces dried mushrooms, preferably porcini or shiitake

1½ cups boiling water

2 tablespoons unsalted butter

1 small onion or large shallot, finely chopped

1 small garlic clove, minced

8 to 10 ounces fresh mushrooms (any kind) cleaned, trimmed, and thinly sliced

¾ cup half-and-half

2 tablespoons quick-dissolving flour, such as Wondra, or as needed

Salt and freshly ground pepper

To prepare the potato *zapekanka*, preheat the oven to 350 degrees F. Grease an 8 x 8-inch baking dish and set aside.

Cook the potatoes in boiling salted water until tender. Drain and immediately pass them through a ricer or food mill placed over a medium bowl. Add the milk, butter, eggs, dill, parsley, salt and pepper and mix well.

Transfer the purée to the prepared baking dish and bake for 30 minutes. If the *zapekanka* has not browned, place under the broiler until the top is light golden brown, about 3 minutes.

Meanwhile, prepare the mushroom sauce. Place the dried mushrooms in a bowl or heatproof measuring cup, add the boiling water, and let them sit for 30 minutes.

Line a small sieve with a wet paper towel, set it over a bowl, and drain the mushrooms in the sieve. Save 1 cup of the liquid. Rinse the mushrooms thoroughly under cool running water to remove any sand or grit, then slice them and set aside (if you do not like the texture of reconstituted dried mushrooms, discard them).

Melt the butter in a nonstick skillet over medium-high heat. Add the onion, reduce the heat slightly, and sauté until light golden, about 7 minutes. Add the garlic and mushrooms and continue to sauté, until the mushrooms are light golden, about 10 minutes more.

Add the half-and-half, the reserved 1 cup mushroom liquid, and the reconstituted mushrooms and stir until hot. Sprinkle the flour over the sauce, stirring constantly, until it reaches the desired thickness. Season to taste with salt and pepper.

Serve this casserole with the sauce on the side.

Valentina's Baptism

As we are on the chapter of ceremonies, I ought to touch upon baptism, which is always performed by immersion. In the rich houses, two tables are laid out in the drawing-room, by the priests; one is covered with holy images, on the other is placed an enormous silver basin, filled with water surrounded by small wax tapers. The chief-priest begins by consecrating the font, and plunging a silver cross repeatedly in the water; he then takes the child, and, after reciting certain prayers, undresses it completely. The process of immersion takes place twice, and so rigorously, that the head must disappear under the water; the infant is then restored to its nurse, and the sacrament is finally administered.

– A description of a baptism in the home of a wealthy nineteenth-century Russian family, from *A Visit to Saint Petersburg in the Winter of 1829–1830*, by Thomas Raikes, Esq., 1838

*I*T WAS A HOT AND MUGGY LATE-SUMMER SUNDAY morning. I awoke at six to catch the metro to Tushinskaya station to meet my friend Lena and her two-year-old daughter, Valentina. Catching a bus near the metro station, we headed to a small town on the outskirts of Moscow where Lena's family has a summer house.

Laden with bags, the three of us piled onto the *avtobus*, which acts as a *dacha* shuttle bus during the summer months. Russians were already packed into the bus. The odor of crowded bodies was nauseating and there was no way to avoid being bathed in some-one else's sweat. Garden tools, bulging sacks, and plants made every inch of the ride a balancing act.

After about one hour of holding onto the upper railing, my knuckles were white and I seemed to have no blood left in my arms. We finally stopped, and the three of us fought our way off the bus. As I caught my breath and realigned my spine, I imagined the return trip, when people would be even sweatier and dirtier after working their land, and the bus even more crowded with bags of apples, potatoes, and other produce going back to the city. But I put my worries aside because today was a special day. Valentina was to be baptized in the local church, and I was to be her godmother.

From the bus stop we proceeded directly to the village church, where Lena went in to inquire about the schedule for baptisms that day. She was told to come back at noon, and if the priests were available, the rite could be performed then.

So off we went with two hours to kill. We walked along the dirt path on the bank of the Moscow River towards Lena's *dacha*, stopping along the way to buy some fresh cow's milk from a neighbor. The broken, peeling fence surrounding the *dacha* was overgrown with weeds, and the branches of apple trees were sagging from the weight of their fruit. Windfall apples littered the ground, providing a feast for the bees. In the hot sun, the back-yard smelled like a cider house.

We changed Valentina into a lacy green dress I had bought in the United States for this special occasion and refreshed ourselves with a glass of juice. Then we made our way back to the church where we met Lena's husband walking up from the bus stop.

We had arrived at the end of Sunday mass, so after the congregation cleared the church, Lena and I placed scarves on our heads and proceeded inside. The stone church was dark and humid but cool, a welcome relief from the midday heat. It was lit only by candles, and the air was thick with incense. Lena asked a woman seated behind a wooden table what items we needed for the baptism service. She replied, 'Three candles and an Orthodox cross.' We bought them. Another mother was behind us in line, waiting to purchase the same items to baptize her two older daughters.

A young priest dressed in a black robe with a bright pink satin sash approached us. We gathered in a circle in front of the altar as he welcomed us into the church. He asked if the two natural mothers of the children were believers. Both mothers shook their heads and quietly whispered, 'No.' A long conversation ensued. The priest asked how they could possibly raise their children to be believers if they themselves were not believers. He then asked if the two godmothers were believers, and we both answered, 'Yes.'

After a lot of fussing and mumbling under his breath, the priest looked up and said, 'My father was a Communist and an atheist, and look at me, I am a priest. Today we have more freedom, the freedom to choose, a freedom that has been denied to us for over seventy years. So, I suppose, you too have the freedom to baptize your children in the Orthodox Church, even if you yourselves are not believers.'

Lena's husband, who is a believer, held Valentina as the service began. A table was set in front of us. On it rested a big copper bowl with three lighted candles on the rim. Warm water was poured into the bowl by the woman who had sold us the candles and the cross, and the priest consecrated it.

The priest began reading a passage from the Bible. He paused, and with a small paintbrush dipped in blessed oil, he painted an X on each child's forehead, neck, and hands. As the priest continued to read, we were told to turn our backs to the altar and face the church door leading outside. With this action, it was explained, we would renounce the devil and force him out of our lives, the children's lives, and the church. As a final blow to the devil, the priest asked the godparents to turn around and symbolically spit towards the door at the retreating devil.

The children undressed, except for their underwear and shoes. Valentina, the youngest, screamed in protest as she was picked up and placed in the copper basin. The priest poured water over her head while chanting and making the sign of the cross. The older girls simply stood near the basin as the priest poured water over their heads and bodies. Small towels were handed out, and the children were dried off and dressed again, this time proudly wearing their crosses on chains around their necks.

The priest cut a snippet of hair from each child's head and placed it in the basin of water. Then he painted more oil on their faces and hands. We lit our candles and walked around the font three times as the priest chanted in a hypnotic voice. After three rounds, the priest picked up each child and carried her to the front of the iconostasis. He lifted each one up and down and from side to side in the shape of a cross.

More oil painting followed, this time with a different oil from that used in the first anointing. Chrism, a special oil usually mixed with balsam and blessed by the head of the Church, was painted on each child and then immediately sponged off by the priest, who was chanting, 'Seal of the Gift of the Holy Spirit.' This painting-then-washing ritual serves as the rite of confirmation, making the child a full member of the Orthodox Church and allowing him or her to receive communion directly after being baptized.

At the end of the service, another young priest, this one holding a large book, walked over to us. He told us the name day, or saint's day, for each child. Valentina's is the 23rd of February.

After the ceremony, we returned to Lena's *dacha*, where we had tea with store-bought cookies that Lena had brought from Moscow. We sat in the garden under the apple trees and talked for hours.

My memory of that day remains vivid. I can still hear the priest's mesmerizing chant and smell the sweet incense and the flickering beeswax candles. Most important, I can still picture a delighted Valentina, twirling around the church in her fancy green dress with her new cross – in a surge of joy that only a two-year-old can freely express.

A Baptism
in Nineteenth-Century Russia

This passage, from *The Russian Peasant*, by Howard Kennard (1907), demonstrates how the baptism ritual performed in the Russian Orthodox Church has changed little over time.

I shall but briefly touch on the subject of baptisms amongst the peasantry. Baptism follows very soon after the birth of a child. At the ceremony, seeing that the little morsel is, so long as it is unchristened, a heathen, the priest first requires it to renounce the devil and all his works. This the baby is naturally unable to do, so the godfather and godmother do it for him, and the church door is opened, that the devil having been dismissed may escape without further contaminating the edifice. The priest turns round and spits at the retreating devil, and the rest of the people then spit likewise, and a prayer from the priest follows ...

Now follows the immersion. The whole party, preceded by the priest and the godfather, make a solemn pilgrimage round the church three times, in the name of the Father, Son, and Holy Ghost. Then the priest consecrates the water and puts a metal cross in it, afterwards immersing the child three times, again in the three sacred names, and lastly bestowing the baptismal name. Then a clean and new white vestment is placed round the child, the priest previously holding the child and the garment on high, and saying: 'Thou, child, art now clean from evil as this shirt!'. . .

After the third immersion the child is a Christian, as a visible sign of which fact the priest suspends a small metal cross to the neck by a black string, and this is kept around the neck as a protective talisman throughout life. The baby is then dressed, the procession is repeated, burning tapers are carried before the child, and it is then anointed with holy oil – body, eyes, ears, mouth, hands, feet – and from four places on its head the priest cuts a piece of silky hair. This is rolled up with a little wax into a ball and thrown into the font.

Russian Name Day Bread
[KRENDEL]

As everybody in Russia was familiar with the Church Calendar, the name day or the Saint's day was celebrated there more than the birth-day (which was observed only by the nearest relatives). On such a day it was the custom, some sixty years ago, to bake several immense *pirogs* [pies] of cake dough; one of these *pirogs* was stuffed with hard-boiled eggs and sometimes also with *kasha*, while the others had no fillings; it was these latter that were sent to various relatives as a sign of affection. When the dinner was served, the remaining *pirog* was brought in and two relatives broke it in half over the head of the person whose name day it was; if the filling fell upon his head, a wish was expressed that gold and silver might fall upon his head in a similar manner; then the *pirog* was divided among those present, who drank vodka to the health of their relative, and then the dinner began in the regular way with the *zakuski*.

Later this custom was modified into simply serving a *pirog* for luncheon, as a first course, after the *zakuski*, and baking a sweet bread in the shape of an eight, which was served for breakfast.

– Nina Nikolaevna Selivanova, *Dining and Wining in Old Russia*

Years ago, this sweet pretzel-shaped yeast-dough coffee cake, called *krendel*, was baked for birthday and name day (or saint's day) celebrations. Name day celebrations were more important than birthday celebrations because they were religious feast days. People were expected to go to church on their name day and then return home to a party, complete with presents.

Name days are not celebrated as they used to be in Old Russia, and *krendel* is not as popular as it once was. But this moist and flavorful coffee cake is particularly good for breakfast, or it can be served as an accompaniment to tea. Though the directions may seem long, they are really quite simple. This bread is even better the second day, after the filling has seeped into the dough.

Sweet Yeast Dough

MAKES 1 LARGE COFFEE CAKE; SERVES 8 TO 10

One ¼-ounce package active dry yeast

½ cup whole milk

2 tablespoons granulated sugar

½ teaspoon salt

8 tablespoons (1 stick) unsalted butter, melted and still warm

1 large egg

1 teaspoon pure vanilla or almond extract

2½ cups all-purpose flour, plus more for rolling out the dough

Nut Filling

8 tablespoons (1 stick) unsalted butter, melted

½ cup lightly packed brown sugar

¼ cup granulated sugar

1½ teaspoons ground cinnamon (optional)

1 cup toasted sliced almonds, chopped walnuts, or pecans

Confectioners' sugar, for dusting

To make the dough, place the yeast in the bowl of an electric mixer or another large mixing bowl.

Heat the milk to lukewarm (about 100 degrees F). Add the milk to the yeast, and gently whisk until the yeast has completely dissolved. Add the sugar, salt, butter, egg, and vanilla and mix until well combined. Add half the flour and mix with the paddle attachment on low speed, or use a wooden spoon, scraping down the sides of the bowl as needed. Add the remaining flour and continue to mix until well incorporated.

To knead the dough with the mixer, increase the speed to medium and mix the dough until it forms a ball. If the dough is too sticky, add a little more flour, 1 tablespoon at a time. Once it forms a ball, continue mixing for 3 minutes.

Or, to knead the dough by hand, generously flour your hands, transfer the dough to a well-floured surface, and form it into a ball. Knead until the dough is soft and supple, about 5 minutes. If the dough sticks to the work surface, add a little more flour, 1 tablespoon at a time. Scrape down the sides of the bowl and return the kneaded dough to the bowl.

Cover the bowl with plastic wrap, and let the dough rise in a warm place for about 1 hour, or until doubled in size.

Line a baking sheet with foil and lightly grease the foil with some of the melted butter; set aside.

Mix the brown sugar and granulated sugar together and set aside.

To roll out the dough, flour the work surface, remove the dough from the bowl, and gently knead it into a ball. Using your hands, flatten the dough into a rectangle, then roll it out to form a 16 x 14-inch rectangle, less than ¼ inch thick. Using a pastry brush, evenly coat the surface of the dough with about 2 tablespoons of the melted butter, then sprinkle it with about 2 tablespoons of the sugar. (If the dough tears at any time during rolling, simply patch it with generously floured hands.)

Fold the dough in half the long way and press it together with your hands. Re-flour the work surface, and roll out the dough to form a 20 x 14-inch rectangle, less than ¼ inch thick. Evenly brush the surface of the dough with about 2 tablespoons of the melted butter and sprinkle with about 2 tablespoons of the sugar. Repeat the procedure one more time. (To prevent the butter and sugar from squirting out, be gentle when rolling out the folded side of the dough.)

Roll out the dough into a long thin rectangle about 28 by 9 inches. Brush the dough with the remaining butter, then sprinkle it with the remaining sugar, the cinnamon, if using, and the nuts. With lightly floured hands, starting at the folded side, roll up the dough into a sausage shape about 1¼ inches thick; it will stretch to about 30 inches long as you roll it up.

Carefully transfer the dough to the prepared baking sheet, seam side down, and form it into an open circle about 8 inches in diameter. Using your fingers, lift and pinch together the edges of the dough to make sure that they are tightly sealed. Gently twist each of the ends to seal their tips, then twist both ends together to form a rope-like tail about 4 inches long. Lift and flip this tail over to form a pretzel shape, and seal the edges of the tail underneath the curve of the pretzel. Place the baking sheet in a warm spot and let the bread rise for 30 minutes.

Position a rack in the center of the oven and preheat the oven to 350 degrees F.

Pinch together any open seams in the dough, then bake for 35 to 40 minutes, until the top is golden brown. Remove the coffee cake from the oven and let cool.

Serve warm or at room temperature. Just before serving, sprinkle the coffee cake with confectioners' sugar. (Any leftovers should be covered and stored at room temperature. Reheat in the oven before serving, if desired.)

Russian Winters

The colder the winter, the sooner the spring will come; the harsher the frost, the hotter the summer; and frequent blizzards in January mean frequent rains in July – rains that are a prerequisite for bountiful mushrooms in August.

– Russian folklore

*T*HE RUSSIANS GREET WINTER WITH MIXED EMOTIONS. The pragmatic side of their character requires that they steel themselves against the hardships they know will come. At the same time, they welcome winter, perhaps from pride in being able to survive its rigors. And, despite the darkness and freezing temperatures, winters in Russia can be invigorating and beautiful.

The first snowfall is always cause for celebration. Moscow comes alive. Pastel green, yellow, pink, and blue buildings are transformed into Impressionist art. Even the heavy concrete Socialist buildings seem to be lightened by a fresh snowfall, and the golden church domes glisten in the sun as if covered with a blanket of diamonds.

The weather is the main topic of conversation at home and on the streets. The colder, the better. Russians actually seem disappointed if the temperature is not below freezing. Apart from being a good excuse to complain, the coldest days tend to be the clearest, and a beautiful azure sky is a tremendous psychological boost in the prevailing gray of winter.

Sunlight is pale and sparse during the long winter months. Daylight, or should I say 'graylight,' does not appear before nine o'clock and the gloomy overcast sky turns black again as early as three-thirty. The darkness can be oppressive, but the Russians do not seem to experience the same depression foreigners do. Perhaps over the centuries they have learned to accept winter's darkness and not to fight it.

Most Russians find great enjoyment in winter sports. People carry their cross-country skis on the metro, headed for the snow-covered forests that surround Moscow. Downhill ski slopes are found in Moscow's Krilatskoye district, about twenty-five minutes from Red Square. Sledding is also popular, and ice hills, slides, and sculptures have appeared for centuries in Moscow's parks.

The Moscow River and small lakes become a social gathering place for ice fishermen. They set up their collapsible canvas camping stools, drill holes in the ice with a corkscrew-like device, and lower their fishing lines into the freezing water. Vodka helps to warm the blood and pass the time. I've never seen anyone catch anything, and I'm not sure whether the fish from such polluted water is for human consumption, cat food, or simply for sport. Perhaps the fishermen just want an excuse to get out of the house for a few hours, away from henpecking wives and mothers-in-law.

Russians regularly plunge into the frozen rivers and swim. After climbing out, bodies steaming in the cold, they do a few jumping jacks in the snow before getting dressed again. Hardy groups, such as the Walrus Club, have made a ritual of ushering in the New Year with a dip in the freezing waters.

Outside Moscow, in the Russian villages, winter is a true test of survival. Villagers spend most of their time indoors, stoking their fires to keep warm, sleeping, or sipping tea. When they go out, they are dressed in high gray felt boots called *valenki*, a sheepskin coat, usually tied with a thick belt at the waist, and a fur hat, or *shapka*. This has been the village winter uniform for centuries and still is today.

During the long winter months, villagers are absolutely dependent on the preparations they made in the summer to ensure enough firewood, food, and clothing. Village markets are empty save for a few root vegetables, and stores carry only the most basic provisions in limited quantities. Salted pickles, cabbage, and tomatoes; dried mushrooms; stored root vegetables; and fruit preserves see the villagers through the darker half of the year.

As winter gives way to spring, usually in early April, everyone breathes a sigh of relief. The snow and ice melt, and the 'mud season' officially begins. Mud is everywhere. You can't escape it. But this temporary, messy inconvenience indicates that the ground is getting soft enough for planting, and soon Russians will re-energize themselves by running their fingers through the earth.

Many Russians get a head start on the growing season by planting tomato seeds in cut-off milk cartons, which they line up on their windowsills. In May, these seedlings are placed on the back window ledges of cars and transported to the countryside, where they will be transplanted, and another Russian growing cycle will begin.

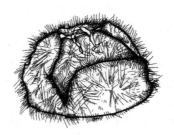

Celebrating Christmas Past and Present

No one in Dikanka saw the devil stealing the moon ... Now what could have prompted the devil to undertake this lawless deed? The reason was this: he knew that the rich Cossack Chub had been invited by the deacon to partake of his Christmas Eve *kutya*, where the guests would include: the headman; a kinsman of the deacon's who sang in the bishop's choir, wearing a blue frockcoat and endowed with a very deep bass; the Cossack Sverbyguz and some other people; where they would sample, besides the traditional Christmas *kutya*, such delights as *varenukha*, vodka infused with saffron, and all sorts of delicacies.

– Nikolay Gogol, *Christmas Eve*

*C*HRISTMAS IS AN EVOLVING TRADITION IN RUSSIA. Since its arrival with Orthodox Christianity during the tenth century, Christmas has gone from being a holy yet somewhat pagan occasion rife with fortune-telling and masked caroling to no occasion at all under Communism. Today Russian Christmas is struggling to redefine itself, and it is currently a mixture of religious observance and secular celebrations.

In 1992, Russia's new government reinstated Christmas as a holiday. Although Russia generally adheres to the Western Gregorian calendar, the government chose the Orthodox Church's Julian date, January 7, as Christmas Day. The Julian calendar runs two weeks behind the Gregorian one, hence January 7 falls fourteen days after December 25. In most Russian minds and homes, Christmas, as a time for tree decorating and gift giving, is celebrated on New Year's Eve – a remnant of Communism's discouragement of religion.

Under the Byzantine Empire, the Christian observance of Christ's birth coincided with the pagan Russian winter festival, *kolyada*. The result was a continuous twelve-day holiday, called *svyatki* (derived from the Russian word for saint) marking both the birth (Christmas, or *Rozhdestvo Khristovo*) and baptism (Epiphany, or *Kreshcheniye*) of Jesus. During *svyatki*, the nobility hosted masquerade balls, while common folk, hidden behind animal masks, went caroling in return for small treats or money, much as American children do on Halloween.

In 1994, the concept of *svyatki* reemerged in Moscow. For the first time, I saw banners proclaiming '*Svyatki 94*' strung across the side streets just off Red Square. A feeble attempt was made to bring back the fair-like atmosphere of yesteryear as small crowds gathered in the square, eating ice cream (despite freezing temperatures), buying souvenirs and balloons, and clapping their hands and shuffling their cold feet to the music of a small band.

For the devout Orthodox, religious observance of Christmas begins on November 28 with a forty-day fast called Saint Phillip's Fast *(Filipovka)*. This fast ends on Christmas Eve, January 6. As with the Great Lent, or Easter Lent, people are not permitted to eat meat or fish and all dairy products are prohibited.

The fast's last day is broken after the midnight Christmas service, a lengthy service that includes Royal Hours (a special liturgy performed only three times a year, the other two times being the eve of the Epiphany and the eve of Good Friday). Like the Easter service, it culminates in the Walk of the Cross, in which the congregation, holding candles, follows the priest in three circuits of the church.

In Old Russia, the feast, or Holy Supper, began when the first star could be seen glimmering in the sky, representing the star the Magi followed to find the Christ child. *Kutya*, a porridge of sweetened wheat berries or rice with honey, nuts, poppy seeds, raisins, or dried fruit, was traditionally the first or last food consumed depending on the customs of the house. Some families set the bowl of *kutya*, with or without a lighted candle placed in the middle of the porridge, on a bed of hay under an icon, symbolic of Christ's birth in a manger. Other families strew hay on top of the dining table, which was then covered with a white cloth.

According to legend, the head of the household threw a spoonful of *kutya* outside for Grandfather Frost, saying, 'Here is a spoonful for thee; please do not touch our crops.' A second spoonful was thrown up onto the ceiling; the grains that stuck prophesied the number of bees there would be in the summer. And lastly, before rising from the table, the members of the household left some *kutya* in their bowls for their departed relatives.

The Christmas season in Russia officially ends on Epiphany, the commemoration of Christ's baptism, twelve days after Christmas. On Epiphany (January 19), the Russian Orthodox Church repeats many of the special services offered for its Christmas service – such as the Royal Hours and a midnight Epiphany Eve service. On the day of Epiphany, the church service usually includes a special ceremony of immersion that is repeated outdoors in nearby rivers, ponds, and other bodies of water in memory of Christ's baptism in the Jordan River.

Today, there is a modest revival of Christmas among Russians, but after all the New Year's Eve excitement, January 7 is almost a letdown. As for December 25, it goes by almost unnoticed – except in 1991, when on Christmas night the Soviet flag was lowered over the Kremlin and seventy-four years of Communist rule came to an end.

Christmas Porridge
[KUTYA]

In pre-Revolutionary Russia, *kutya*, a sweet porridge akin to rice pudding, was traditionally served on two occasions – as part of the Christmas feast and at funeral celebrations. At Russian funerals, spoonfuls of the porridge are thrown into the gravesite during the burial, or a bowl of *kutya* is left on the grave of the departed.

There are many recipes for *kutya*, most of them calling for either rice or wheat berries as the main ingredient, along with raisins, poppy seeds, almonds, and honey. Sometimes a compote made from dried or fresh fruit is served as an accompaniment to *kutya*.

This is my mother's recipe for *kutya*, which she learned from her mother. It is made with soaked wheat berries boiled in water, rinsed, and then mixed with pan-browned flour and sliced almonds, raisins, sugar, and cinnamon (a Western addition). The *kutya* is placed in a bowl and decorated with more raisins around the edges, and a cross is made in the middle with whole blanched almonds. You can adjust the amount of sugar and cinnamon to suit your taste. Served with a touch of cream, *kutya* is great for breakfast.

Wheat berries are available in health food stores and most whole food stores. There are two kinds: soft wheat berries, which are small, round, and red, and hard wheat berries, which are longer and golden. Use the second kind for this dish.

SERVES 6 TO 8

1 cup golden wheat berries (see above)

3 tablespoons all-purpose flour

⅓ cup sliced almonds

¼ teaspoon ground cinnamon, or to taste

½ cup sugar, or to taste

½ cup golden or dark raisins, soaked in boiling water to soften
   them and drained
2 tablespoons dark raisins, for garnish (optional)
7 whole blanched almonds, for garnish (optional)
Heavy cream, for serving (optional)

Rinse the wheat berries. Soak them in a bowl of water for 12 hours, or overnight. Drain.

Bring 1 quart water to a boil in a 2-quart saucepan. Add the soaked wheat berries, reduce the heat, and skim off any foam. Gently simmer, uncovered, until the grains are tender, about 2½ hours. (The outer skins will remain a bit tough.) Rinse the wheat berries under cold running water, then transfer them to a large bowl, and set aside.

Combine the flour and sliced almonds in a small nonstick skillet and place over medium-high heat. Stir constantly with a wooden spoon and shake the pan occasionally until the flour is light golden and the almonds are lightly toasted, about 7 minutes. Do not let the flour burn or it will have a bitter taste.

Add the flour and the sliced almonds to the wheat berries, along with the cinnamon, sugar, and golden raisins. Mix until well blended. Let the *kutya* sit at room temperature for 2 hours before serving; stir occasionally.

Transfer the *kutya* to a serving bowl. If using them, arrange the dark raisins around the edge of the bowl, then make a cross shape in the middle with the whole almonds. Serve at room temperature. Pass the cream at the table, if desired.

A Black–Tie
New Year's Eve Celebration

My dear _____ ,

Yesterday was the Russian New Year's Day: it was celebrated by a fête which can be seen in no other country; it is a fête original, extraordinary, and characteristic of the nation. The sovereign and his family commence the new year by an assembly given to the people; not less than twenty-five thousand invitations are issued to this gigantic rout. At seven o'clock in the evening the doors of the Winter Palace of the Hermitage are thrown open to the multitude: the innumerable rooms are lighted up with myriads of [*sic*] wax candles; at convenient distances are placed side-boards with refreshments, adorned with pyramids of gold and silver plate; bands of military music resound in every corner to amuse the ear . . . And for whom was this colossal entertainment prepared? For every rank and degree; from the highest noble to the lowest peasant, all were equally welcome without distinction to pay their respects at the foot of the throne . . .

— Thomas Raikes's *A Visit to St. Petersburg in the Winter of 1829–1830*, describing a New Year's celebration hosted by Emperor Nicholas I (1825–1855) at the Winter Palace of the Hermitage in St. Petersburg

*R*USSIAN NEW YEAR'S CELEBRATIONS, which begin on December 31 and continue into the late hours of January 1, have been consistently raucous for centuries. The Communists, who all but stamped out Christmas, encouraged New Year's revelry.

Russians traditionally decorate their Christmas trees, called *yolki*, on December 31, just before the New Year. Garbed in a long red robe with a white rope-like sash, *Ded Moroz*, or Father Frost, can be seen wandering about town accompanied by his granddaughter, the beautiful *Snegurochka*, or Snow Maiden, who is dressed in a pastel blue gown glimmering with white sequin snowflakes and crowned with a snowflake tiara. Together they visit children on New Year's Eve, when gifts are exchanged.

Until 1992, it was possible for parents in Moscow to call a local number to order a private visit from *Ded Moroz* on New Year's Eve. They would arrange a time, and *Ded Moroz* would appear at the door. The children were told to wait in the living room while the parents gave Father Frost the presents they had bought for their children. Some people say this service still exists, but at an exorbitant cost.

Ded Moroz would arrive and greet the children, chat with them, and ask them to sing, dance, or recite a poem in exchange for their gifts. Undoubtedly, he would share a toast of vodka with each family, making early visits more desirable. By the end of the night, after many festive house calls, *Ded Moroz* would be in no shape to entertain the kids. My friend Anna told me that one time, when she was young, *Ded Moroz* simply didn't show up at the scheduled time. He did, however, appear the next morning, but his condition was so unpresentable he had to be turned away at the door.

Today, apart from private house calls, *Ded Moroz* and his snowflake sidekick make a scheduled annual appearance at the Kremlin Palace, where ballet, puppet shows, and theater productions benefit Moscow's young. Colorfully dressed elves line the walkway to the Kremlin Theater, where hundreds of excited children, dressed in their Sunday best, are greeted at the door and given small gifts and wrapped candies.

For adults in Moscow, Red Square, like Times Square in New York, comes alive on New Year's Eve. Floodlights are ablaze and banners proclaiming 'Happy New Year,' *'S Novym Godom'* in Russian, are strung across the streets. White Christmas tree lights decorate the trees in nearby Manezh Square in front of the Bolshoi Theater, and a huge Christmas tree decorated with colored lights stands to the side of the world-famous onion domes of St. Basil's Cathedral.

Every year thousands of people, Muscovites and foreigners alike, jam the square. At the magic hour, when the Kremlin bells chime midnight, people make their holiday wishes, champagne corks are popped, toasts are made, *'S Novym Godom'* is shouted, and empty champagne and vodka bottles are smashed on the icy cobblestones. Dressed in their warmest clothing, Russians openly rejoice. Hugs and kisses are exchanged between friends and strangers alike. A warm fog rises from the ground as people sing, dance, stomp their feet, and jump up and down to keep warm. Overhead, fireworks explode, creating a brilliant kaleidoscope in the sky.

This joyous celebration lasts for no more than thirty minutes. The ice-cold wind whipping up from the Moscow River and the snow flurries drive people to shelter. Within half an hour, Red Square clears out as people return to their warm homes to continue celebrating.

On New Year's Eve of 1992, I was fortunate to be invited to my friend Anna's house. She lived with her parents, younger sister, and her grandmother in a beautiful old high-ceilinged apartment on Kutuzovsky Prospekt. The invitation read 11:00 P.M., so at 10:45 I left my apartment to walk to Anna's house on what seemed to be the coldest night of the year. Snow was falling steadily, muffling all noise except the crunch of dry snow underfoot. After fifteen minutes in the cold, my face was red and chapped and my nose frozen.

Anna answered the door, bubbly as ever and elegantly dressed. She invited me in and we exchanged the traditional triple-cheek Russian kiss. One cardinal rule in Russia is that greetings are never exchanged over the threshold of the door. Guests must have both feet in your home before you welcome them, shake hands, or kiss.

After completing the winter ritual of taking off layers of clothing, and removing my hat and boots, I entered the living room to be greeted by a crowd of people. I suddenly realized that this was a black-tie dinner, a rare phenomenon in Russia. An enormous tree stood in the corner of the room, beautifully decorated with German ornaments. A Russian-style Santa Claus doll was holding court at the base of the tree. As I said hello to everyone, one guest handed me a slip of paper with a number on it, for the door prizes we would receive later in the evening.

A beautifully set large table stood in the middle of the room, laden with enough food to feed fifty people, instead of the twenty who were there. As usual, the *zakuska* course was on the table. Bowls, plates, and platters were piled high. Meat-filled *pirozhki*, *salat Olivier*, pastry cups filled with liver pâté, turkey loaf with pistachio nuts, *kholodets* (jellied pork) with horseradish

sauce (tinted pink with beet juice), eggs stuffed with caviar, smoked sturgeon and salmon, salami and other cold cuts, a mushroom and onion casserole, chicken *satsivi* (a spicy Georgian chicken dish flavored with cilantro and walnuts), salted cabbage, and a large platter of pickled vegetables – green onions, garlic, peppers and cabbage – all resting on sprigs of fresh cilantro, parsley, and dill.

Five minutes before midnight, our host turned on the television. Bottles of sparkling wine were opened, their contents spraying in all directions, and we filled our glasses. At the stroke of midnight, signaled by the Kremlin chimes, everyone stood up and toasted the New Year. The lights were turned off, and we lit sparklers, exchanging jubilant hugs and kisses.

Just as we finished the *zakuski* there was a knock at the door. A Georgian neighbor invited the entire party outside for a display of fireworks and a swig of vodka. We put on our coats and boots and trudged to the far end of the parking lot, where a large man dressed as *Ded Moroz* acted as the master of ceremonies. He set off fireworks and lit sparklers in between vodka toasts and bites of *khvorost*, or crisp deep-fried cookies in the shape of twigs, sprinkled with powdered sugar to resemble snow-covered forest branches. Another young man played the guitar while everyone sang Russian folk songs. All the excitement and vodka kept us warm and indifferent to the freezing temperatures. After the last fireworks were set off, our party retreated to the dining room table to attack the spread of *zakuski* yet again.

As we ate, one of the guests disappeared from the living room, reappearing moments later in a rooster outfit – 1993 being the Year of the Rooster. Everyone howled with laughter and glasses were immediately raised to toast the rooster, who was garbed in shorts, a T-shirt with 1993 printed across the front, green flippers, a fluorescent green bathing cap with an orange cockscomb, and a feather duster for a tail.

I joined the handful of women who disappeared into the kitchen to work on the main course and chat. The other guests danced, sang, and played games. The numbers we had drawn earlier corresponded to small tokens – lipsticks, pens, address books, hair clips, and the like – which were distributed with great ceremony. At three o'clock in the morning, the main course was finally served, broiled tenderloin of beef with oven-browned potatoes and individual mushroom casseroles called *zhulyen*. The toasting resumed.

As a rule, Russians do not make New Year's resolutions. Instead, they make endless toasts, alternating between champagne and vodka. They toast to each other, to good times to come, and to hardships they hope to leave behind. One toast was testament to their country's recent metamorphosis: 'To Russia! Last year we didn't know what to call our country – no longer the Soviet Union. This year we do – Russia. And we will always hold Russia dear in our hearts.'

I was in a food (and vodka) coma by the time dessert was served at five. Three kinds of cakes, called *torty*, cookies, and fruit compote completed the feast. The Georgian neighbors and their entourage of guests returned – with a guitar. Coffee was made and tea was served from a samovar. Even more neighbors showed up to spread the good cheer, and the merrymaking continued until seven, when the first guests started to leave, while others simply found a comfortable spot to fall asleep.

Not surprisingly, the streets of Moscow are deserted on January 1. All stores and restaurants are closed, and people are too tired or too hung over to function. Street cleaners, usually older women so heavily bundled they can barely move, pick up broken glass and other debris from the cobblestones of Red Square. And so begins another year – what it will hold is anyone's guess, especially in Russia.

Eggplant Caviar

Eggplant caviar, also known as poor man's caviar, derives its name from the tiny seeds in the eggplant that separate during the cooking process. I like to think of it as Russian guacamole, especially the baked version. In Russia, you can buy eggplant caviar in a can, but it's a bit too tomatoey and acidic for my taste.

I have given two recipes here for eggplant caviar – a stovetop version, in which all the ingredients are simmered together in a saucepan, and a baked version, in which the eggplant is baked, and then the pulp is removed and combined with chopped fresh tomatoes, green onions, and cilantro. Either version is a great appetizer served on crackers or crispy toasts – and, like guacamole, the baked version is particularly good with tortilla chips.

Stovetop Eggplant Caviar

[TUSHONAYA BAKLAZHANNAYA IKRA]

SERVES 6 TO 8

⅓ cup olive oil

1 small sweet onion (such as Vidalia), finely chopped

1 large (1½ pounds) purple eggplant, peeled and cut into
¼-inch dice or smaller

1 small garlic clove, minced

One 14.5-ounce can diced tomatoes, drained

3 tablespoons tomato paste

1 teaspoon salt

3 tablespoons chopped fresh cilantro or dill, or a combination

Heat the olive oil in a 3-quart saucepan over medium-high heat until hot. Add the onion and sauté, stirring occasionally, until light golden, about 5 minutes. Add the eggplant and garlic (do not stir), cover, and cook for 3 minutes to allow the eggplant to release some of its juices so it will not absorb too much oil.

Stir the eggplant and onion until well combined, then reduce the heat to low and gently simmer, uncovered, for 5 minutes. Add the diced tomatoes, tomato paste, and salt and continue to simmer, stirring about every 5 minutes, until the eggplant is soft and the sauce is thick, about 15 minutes.

If serving hot, transfer the eggplant caviar to a serving dish, garnish with the cilantro, and serve immediately. The dish can also be served at room temperature. (Cover and refrigerate any leftovers.)

Baked Eggplant Caviar

[PECHONAYA BAKLAZHANNAYA IKRA]

SERVES 6

Canola oil, for greasing the baking sheet
1 large (1½ pounds) purple eggplant, rinsed and green top cut off
1 large ripe tomato, seeded and cut into small dice
1 tiny garlic clove, minced
1 tablespoon fresh lemon juice, or to taste
1 green onion, green part only, thinly sliced
2 tablespoons chopped fresh cilantro or dill
2 tablespoons chopped walnuts, toasted (optional)
Salt and freshly ground pepper to taste

Preheat the oven to 450 degrees F. Line a baking sheet with foil and generously grease the foil with canola oil.

Cut the eggplant lengthwise in half. Using a sharp knife, make ½-inch-deep diagonal crisscross incisions on the cut side of each half. Arrange the eggplant halves cut side down on the baking sheet and bake until the pulp is soft and the skins are browned, 25 to 30 minutes. Test the softness of the pulp by inserting the tip of a knife through the eggplant skin. Remove the eggplant from the oven, and let cool slightly.

Using a spoon, scrape the eggplant pulp from the skin onto a chopping board. Chop it until it reaches a chunky purée consistency (do *not* use a food processor). Transfer the pulp to a serving bowl, add the remaining ingredients, and mix until well incorporated. Adjust seasoning and serve immediately; or cover and refrigerate until ready to serve. (The eggplant caviar can be made 1 day in advance.)

Potatoes Russian–Style

Like cabbage, potatoes are a year-round staple in Russia. Straight from the ground, a Russian potato is a special treat. Potatoes are planted in late spring, harvested in August, and stored in cellars or under the floorboards of village homes. In the city, Russians store potatoes on their balconies, when the temperatures freeze, they bring them in and hide them in a dark, dry closet. With any luck, the potatoes will not sprout or turn green, and they will remain edible until late May, when the planting cycle begins again.

Russian potatoes are among the tastiest in the world, and, unlike those in the United States, they do not come in endless, confusing varieties. The simple, standard Russian potato boils perfectly, fries beautifully, and bakes nicely. Some American grocery stores carry Russian fingerling potatoes. These banana-shaped tubers have a smooth waxy texture and a sweet taste. They are delicious in the following potato dishes. For the first recipe, boil the potatoes whole, then slice them before mixing with the butter, herbs, and garlic. For the second, do not peel the fingerling potatoes before sautéing. Either recipe makes a perfect side dish.

Boiled Potatoes with Fresh Herbs

[VARYONY KARTOFEL S TRAVOY]

When it comes to boiling potatoes, most Russians simply boil them in water until tender, but others go through a special ritual that is quite entertaining. I was first introduced to the ritual by my friend Natalya, and then I saw it on a Russian cooking program on TV. The procedure basically involves boiling the potatoes, draining them and returning them to the pot, then adding butter, minced garlic, parsley, salt, and pepper, covering the pot, and swinging it around for about three minutes, or until the potatoes are slightly bruised, which allows the butter to seep in. Then the pot is wrapped in a woolen blanket (intended to prevent the steam from escaping) and left to sit on the counter or floor for twenty minutes before serving. I have slightly modified this unique Russian technique by wrapping the pot in plastic wrap and then covering it with a thick dish towel.

SERVES 4

1½ pounds baby Yukon Gold, white, or red potatoes, scrubbed
Salt
2 tablespoons unsalted butter
3 tablespoons chopped fresh parsley, dill, or cilantro, or a combination of any of your favorite fresh herbs
1 small garlic clove, minced
Freshly ground pepper

Put the potatoes in a large saucepan and add enough water just to cover them. Add 2 teaspoons salt, cover, and bring to a boil. Reduce the heat slightly and cook just until the potatoes are tender, 15 to 20 minutes, depending on the size of the potatoes.

Drain the potatoes and immediately return them to the warm saucepan. Add the butter, parsley, garlic, and salt and pepper to taste. Replace the lid and, holding the lid on tightly, gently swirl and shake the potatoes to slightly break them and allow the butter, parsley, and garlic to seep in. Wrap the covered saucepan in plastic wrap to prevent steam from escaping and place a large thick dish towel on top, if you wish. Let the potatoes sit for about 15 minutes before serving.

Unwrap and uncover the saucepan, and serve the potatoes.

Sautéed Potatoes with Wild Mushrooms

[ZHARENY KARTOFEL S GRIBAMI]

Sautéed potatoes are a classic side dish for meat, poultry, or fish. Though many recipes call for boiling the potatoes before frying them, I find that if my skillet is at the right temperature, the potatoes are tender and perfectly browned without parboiling.

SERVES 4

3 tablespoons olive oil

1 medium onion, cut in half and thinly sliced

1½ pounds Yukon Gold potatoes, peeled and cut into ⅛-inch slices

8 ounces mushrooms (any kind), cleaned, trimmed, and sliced

1 tablespoon unsalted butter

1 small garlic clove, minced

Dash of paprika (optional)

Salt and freshly ground pepper

2 tablespoons chopped fresh parsley, for garnish

Heat the oil in a large heavy-bottomed nonstick skillet over medium-high heat. Add the onion and sauté until translucent, about 3 minutes. Add the potatoes, stirring to mix with the onions, reduce the heat slightly, and sauté for 10 minutes.

Add the mushrooms and butter and continue to sauté until the potatoes are tender and golden brown. About every 3 minutes, toss and mix the potatoes and mushrooms with a wide spatula.

Add the garlic, paprika, if using, and salt and pepper to taste and continue to cook for 3 minutes. Remove from the heat, adjust the seasoning, and garnish with the parsley. Serve immediately.

Individual Mushroom Casseroles
[ZHULYEN]

These tasty little mushroom casseroles are a standard appetizer on most Russian restaurant menus. Piping hot, straight from the oven, they arrive at the table in long-handled individual decorative copper pans or in simple ceramic ramekins. *Zhulyen* can be made with any fresh mushroom, but the more flavorful varieties, such as shiitake, chanterelle, or porcini are particularly good. These casseroles can be served as a first course or as a side dish to accompany meat, poultry, or fish. They can be assembled a day in advance, refrigerated, and then baked just before serving.

SERVES 4 TO 5

2 tablespoons unsalted butter
1 pound mushrooms (any kind), cleaned, trimmed, and cut into
   quarters or sixths, depending on their size
1 small garlic clove, minced
2 tablespoons thinly sliced fresh chives
½ cup sour cream
3 tablespoons chopped fresh parsley
Salt and freshly ground pepper
¾ cup (3 ounces) grated Gruyère

Preheat the oven to 425 degrees F.

Melt the butter in a large heavy skillet over medium heat. Add the mushrooms and sauté, stirring, until most of the liquid they release has evaporated and the mushrooms are nicely browned, about 10 minutes. Stir in the chives and remove from the heat.

Stir in the sour cream and parsley and season to taste with salt and pepper. Divide the mushrooms among 4 or 5 ovenproof ramekins placed on a baking sheet. Sprinkle the top of each one liberally with the Gruyère cheese.

Bake until bubbly and the tops are well browned, about 15 minutes. Serve immediately.

Snow Cookies
[KHVOROST]

Just about every country has at least one recipe for fried dough, and Russia is no exception. The Russian name for these cookies, *khvorost*, which means 'twig' or 'small branch,' is apt, because when they are sprinkled with powdered sugar, the little morsels resemble a pile of sticks covered with snow. There is very little sugar in the dough, so be generous with the confectioners' sugar on top. A sprinkle of cinnamon is a nice touch, although not Russian. These cookies make a festive and tasty addition to any holiday table.

MAKES ABOUT 80 COOKIES
1¾ cups plus 2 tablespoons all-purpose flour
½ teaspoon baking powder
Pinch of salt
2 large eggs

2 tablespoons granulated sugar
4 tablespoons (½ stick) unsalted butter, softened
1 tablespoon Grand Marnier, brandy, or vodka
2 teaspoons pure vanilla or almond extract
Canola oil, for deep-frying
Confectioners' sugar, for dusting the finished cookies

Sift the flour, baking powder, and salt into a small bowl.

Combine the eggs and granulated sugar in a medium mixing bowl and beat with an electric mixer on medium speed for 2 minutes. Add the butter and half the flour mixture and beat until combined, then add the remaining flour and beat until the dough comes together. Add the Grand Marnier and continue beating until the dough forms a ball. Wrap the ball in plastic wrap and refrigerate for at least 2 hours, or overnight.

Bring the covered dough to room temperature. Have ready a baking sheet lined with parchment paper for the formed cookies before frying, and a plate lined with paper towels ready for the finished cookies. Cut the dough in half, and, on a lightly floured work surface, roll out one portion ⅛ inch thick. With a pastry wheel or a sharp knife, cut into rectangular strips about ¾ inch wide and 2 inches long. Cut a 1-inch vertical slit down the center of each strip, then twist one end of the rectangle through the hole, forming a loose loop. Place the formed cookies on the prepared baking sheet. Repeat the procedure with the remaining dough.

In a large deep pot or deep-fryer, heat the oil to 350 to 375 degrees F. Fry the dough pieces, in batches, until light golden brown and cooked through, about 30 seconds on each side. (Let the oil reheat between batches.) Drain on the paper towels, then arrange the fried cookies on a serving platter and very generously dust with confectioners' sugar.

Russian Weddings

The only guest from town was my sister, to whom Masha had sent a note a couple of days before the wedding; she wore a white dress and gloves. During the ceremony she cried softly for joy, being deeply touched, and her expression was motherly, infinitely kind. Our happiness had intoxicated her and she smiled continually, as if inhaling heady fumes. Watching her during the service I realized that for her there was nothing finer in the whole world than earthly love.

– Anton Chekhov, *My Life*

CIVIL CEREMONIES ARE BY FAR THE MOST POPULAR MEANS of exchanging marriage vows in Russia, although church weddings, while still rare, are making a comeback. Romance and weddings are modern affairs, influenced by the fast pace of contemporary urban life and the impersonal bureaucracy of government. Ancient traditions and rituals that were once popular in the countryside have been largely forgotten or left behind by those who have moved to the city to find work and love. Nonetheless, the traditional feast that follows the wedding ceremony is as popular today as it was centuries ago.

The dating scene in Russia is similar to the dating scene around most of the globe. Young couples can be seen gazing into each others' eyes and smooching on bridges and park benches, or at restaurants and bars – just about anywhere outside their crowded homes, away from the chaos of extended families living in two-room apartments where privacy is nonexistent. If American teenagers think they have no privacy, just imagine how their Russian counterparts must feel, sharing the same room with their siblings or, even worse, their grandmothers.

Bringing your girlfriend or boyfriend home to meet mom and dad is the last thing young couples do before getting married. And forget about asking the girl's parents for their daughter's hand in marriage. Most Russian men 'pop the question' casually, and I am told that sometimes they skip proposing marriage entirely and ask the girl only for a marriage date. Engagements are usually short. Diamond engagement rings are rarely given, but engagement parties are quite popular, especially among the bridegroom and his friends.

Once a young couple, usually in their early twenties, decides to get married, they must start the bureaucratic ball rolling at least two months before their wedding date. This two- or three-month grace period is supposedly to guard against rushed decisions, but, given the high divorce rate in Russia, it is obviously ineffective.

Two months prior to the wedding date, both partners are required to go to a registry office that deals with changes of civilian status, called *ZAGS* in Russian *(Zapis Aktov Grazhdanskogo Sostoyaniya)*, where they must present their internal passports and any divorce documents, if necessary. After paying a small fee, they receive a piece of paper stating that they have officially registered their request to get married. The date of their wedding is then scheduled.

Each district in Moscow has at least one such office, where all marriages, church or civil, must be registered, and where civil ceremonies are conducted in an assembly-line fashion. No health documents or blood tests are required to get married – it is assumed that each partner is knowledgeable about the other's health. The minimum marriage age is eighteen. *ZAGS* is also the place where births, divorces, and deaths are registered.

Unlike the Orthodox Church, which imposes numerous restrictions, these halls are open for civil weddings throughout the week, regardless of holy days. The most popular days, of course, are Fridays and Saturdays. Church weddings, on the other hand, can never take place on fast days or holy days, which make up about one-third of the year.

Sometimes the prospective bride and groom meet their future in-laws only after they have registered to get married. The in-laws then meet each other and begin planning the wedding reception and working out the finances. There are no set traditions regarding which side of the family pays for what. The total cost is usually split, or the wealthier family foots the bill. Mothers are the party planners, and unless families can afford the exorbitant price of a hotel or restaurant reception, the party takes place at home.

There is no traditional menu for wedding feasts. Most receptions start with a lavish array of *zakuski* – sturgeon caviar, eggplant caviar, fresh salads, smoked fish, jellied meat *(kholodets)*, sautéed mushrooms, and of course, lightly salted cucumbers (for the toasts), followed by soup (usually *shchi*) and pies filled with meat or cabbage and hard-boiled eggs, or filled with fish (in which case they are called *kulebyaka*), or with chicken *(kurnik)*. Braised meat and potatoes follow, and a simple dessert, perhaps a store-bought cake or two, is served with coffee or tea to end the meal. The traditional tiered wedding cakes common in America do not exist in Russia. *Karavay*, a special wedding bread, is usually consumed sometime before or during dinner. Small souvenirs for all the guests are provided at each place setting – usually a little white cloth filled with chocolates or candies and tied with ribbon.

Under Communism, when a couple registered their wedding at *ZAGS*, they received a special distribution card that gave them access to special shops where certain items otherwise impossible to buy in bulk could be obtained. These included black and red caviar, smoked sturgeon and other smoked fish, champagne and vodka, and other party food. These cards no longer exist, and today people spend weeks shopping around, trying to gather all the necessary ingredients to put together a large wedding feast.

On the day of the wedding, the bride's mother and girl-friends help her get dressed at home. The rest of the wedding party, or those who will be present at the ceremony, usually assemble at the groom's home. During the nineteenth century, in his book *Russian People* (1880), Zabylin writes, 'On the wedding day, the bride ties some bark to her waist (to protect her from attack); she places some flax and soap under her armpit (in hopes that her possessor will be rich and clean); and finally, she places some small knotted cakes on her breasts (so that her family will always have an abundance of bread and milk and they will always lead well-nourished lives).' These traditions did not survive the twentieth century.

From the groom's house, the wedding party goes to pick up the bride. Some charming remnants of old, lost traditions are still practiced today. For instance, sometimes the groom, and only the groom, knocks on the front door. The mother of the bride traditionally opens the door and the groom then asks how much the bride will cost him. He begins throwing money on the ground, starting with small bills, and when his mother-in-law thinks there is enough money, she hands over her daughter to him. This is a dowry in reverse – the groom paying for the bride instead of the bride's parents paying the groom to marry their daughter.

The newlyweds' car (usually a rented Russian limousine or a foreign car) and all of the other cars in the wedding motorcade are decorated – a colorful if perhaps tacky ritual. Pink, blue, and white ribbons, and sometimes plastic flowers, are draped across the hoods of the cars giving them a wrapped-gift box appearance.

A fixture of two interlocking circles with bells inside is attached to the top of the newlyweds' car, and occasionally a plastic doll is fixed to the front grill – a weird and somewhat disturbing sight.

From the bride's house, the young couple piles into their decorated car, leaving their parents behind to prepare for the post-*ZAGS* feast. Many Russian parents do not attend their children's weddings – a custom that dates back as far as the sixteenth century. The bride receives armfuls of bouquets from her friends, which she leaves in their cellophane wrapping to be placed on Russian monuments during photo opportunities later on.

On a crisp autumn day, Dmitry and Ksenya, friends of my friend Anna (one of the hostesses for the New Year's Eve celebration), were married at *ZAGS*. Our wedding party, along with numerous others, gathered in a large, stuffy, smoky waiting room with mirrored walls, beige sofas and chairs, artificial banana trees, and bright-pink bougainvillea plants. In one corner was a desk with a computer, where couples registered and purchased their marriage certificates. Clusters of brides and grooms were standing around nervously, waiting for their names to be called. The brides, most dressed in rented almost-see-through polyester wedding dresses, were understandably jittery. Some were basking in the limelight on their big day, but others desperately tried to avoid it, as was the case with one bride who was conspicuously pregnant. Their future spouses wore mostly suits and ties – but not the traditional red banner across their chests that was required under Communism.

A rough-looking middle-aged man carrying a clipboard called out the names. Once called, the conveyor-belt wedding process began. Our party was told to stand on a red carpet outside a large set of wooden doors. From the other side of the doors we could hear a string quartet playing some marching music as a just-married couple walked toward the door. The music stopped, the doors opened, and literally two minutes later, our party was walking down the same red carpet and being serenaded by the same quartet. Apparently the live string quartet, however tired-sounding, is a class above the standard scratchy tape-recorded wedding music played in most *ZAGS*.

Ksenya carried a bouquet of white lilies and red carnations. She and Dmitry stood first in line, followed by their best man and bridesmaid, and then the rest of the guests. Once the whole party was inside the room, the doors closed and the couple and best couple went to the front of the room. The rest of us stood in the back. The room was decorated with gaudy tie-dyed beige-blue curtains that had glittery gold bells painted on them. On one wall hung a large Soviet-era social-realist work of art depicting a couple working together in a field.

In front of the curtain backdrop was a large, high white-and-robin-egg-blue table decorated with the symbolic interlocking gold wedding circles. On this table stood a vase of fresh roses, and at the far end was a notebook that the couple and their witnesses would sign later. A young woman with dark brown hair, wearing a brown knit dress and shocking-pink Wizard-of-Oz-like shoes, presided over the ceremony. In a monotonous voice, she said a few words about the institution of marriage. Then the couple quickly exchanged their vows. The officiant asked the couple and the best couple to sign their names in the notebook, pointing to the proper line with a clear lucite wand.

The couple exchanged rings, which are worn on the ring finger of the right hand in Russia, not the left. If a person wears his or her ring on the left hand, it usually indicates that he or she is divorced. The couple exchanged a kiss, the officiant said a few more words, and it was over. From start to finish, the ceremony took less than ten minutes.

The quartet struck up again and the couple walked back down the red carpet and out the doors, followed by the rest of us.

As we left, the next wedding party was gathered on the other side of the doors, eagerly awaiting its cue.

After the wedding ceremony is over, most wedding parties proceed directly to a TV-video monitor set up in the waiting room area of *ZAGS* where they can watch a videotape of their wedding – either to buy it, or simply to see an instant replay. Perhaps it is a good thing to have a tape, because everything happens so quickly one might need to see it again to believe it.

The members of our party left *ZAGS* and got into their decorated cars to make the rounds of the monuments. These 'monument rounds' are a vital part of any wedding day. Every day, and at any time of day, one can see couples visiting monuments such as the Tomb of the Unknown Soldier, St. Basil's Cathedral and Red Square, Lenin Hills, Novodevichy Monastery, the White House (Parliament Building), the World War II Monument Park on Kutuzovsky Prospekt, and sometimes even a Russian Orthodox church. The bride leaves one of her many cellophane-wrapped bouquets at the base of each monument, and bottles of champagne are popped open as the toasting and fun begin.

These stops can involve so much merrymaking that some couples have been known to miss their actual wedding receptions. But most wedding parties eventually end up at the reception, where they are greeted at the door by both couple's parents. Traditionally, one of the mothers offers the newlyweds a loaf of bread, called *karavay*, with a small saltcellar on top, while the other mother holds an icon – both symbols of the hoped-for health, happiness, and prosperity of a new home. Some couples follow ancient traditions and immediately bite into the bread. It is believed that whoever gets the larger chunk of bread in his or her mouth will dominate the household.

After the bread ritual, the feasting begins. Toasts are *de rigueur.* The first toast is always to the newlyweds. During the remainder of the meal, whenever anyone yells out, *'Gorko!'* (which means

'Bitter!'), the newlyweds must stop whatever they are doing and kiss the bitterness out of their lives. This wonderful custom sometimes prevents the couple from getting much to eat, or from having anything to say.

Traditional wedding gifts include household items, especially if the couple is lucky enough to move into their own apartment – a very rare occurrence in Russia. Or a couple may receive money, which usually goes toward their honeymoon. After getting married, most young couples move in with one set of parents and are given one room in the apartment to call their own.

Weddings in the Orthodox Church are the opposite of the short, utilitarian *ZAGS* ceremonies. They are lavish, coronation-like occasions, lasting about three hours. The couple getting married goes through the ancient rituals of lighting candles, having crowns held above their heads, kissing icons, drinking wine from the chalice, exchanging blessed rings, and walking around the altar three times. The soft candlelight, the sweet smell of incense, and the inspiring chanting create a beautiful and emotional occasion – a far cry from the impersonal assembly-line scene at *ZAGS*. But a couple married in an Orthodox Church still has to visit the local *ZAGS* to register their marriage.

Outside big cities such as Moscow and St. Petersburg, weddings are usually not so complicated or elaborate. Village

weddings, in fact, are a rarity. Many young people living in the countryside are forced to move to the city to find work and a partner.

Unlike contemporary marriages, in which parents have little or no say in their children's wedding plans, marriages of yesteryear used to be arranged either by the parents of the bride or by the village matchmaker, called a *svakha*. The bride and groom had no control of their destiny, and frequently were not allowed to see each other before walking down the aisle. Hence, the Russian word for bride, *nevesta*, may stem from *neizvestnaya*, 'unknown.'

In these arranged marriages, the families of the young couple almost always knew each other. Together they organized the bride's dowry, which consisted of bed linens, household items, garments, jewelry, servants, livestock, money, and property, and they made arrangements for engagement parties and the wedding feast. The young bride, usually thirteen to fifteen years old, was looked upon as an addition to the workforce, and if she was pretty, that was a matter of luck.

Like much of Russian life, ancient wedding traditions were rife with superstition and symbols. For instance, the person whose foot touched the carpet first in church, or the one whose candle had the higher flame, was destined to be the boss of the household. Also, at the wedding reception, after the couple drank from the same cup, the groom smashed the cup on the floor so that no one could ever make another toast from the same cup. Grain, symbolizing fertility, was traditionally sprinkled on the married couples as they left the church, and their seats at the wedding feast were covered with sable or other fur, symbolizing future wealth. The couple's bedroom and bed linens were exorcised by a matchmaker, and a family icon was nailed above the newlyweds' bed. When the bride and groom exchanged gifts, he usually gave her a sewing kit or toiletries, and she gave him a whip. Luckily, times have changed.

Meat-Filled Dumplings from Siberia
[SIBIRSKIYE PELMENY]

Pelmeny, meat-filled dumplings shaped like tortellini, were first introduced to Russia by Mongol invaders during the thirteenth century. Needless to say, *pelmeny* are more than just dumplings to the Russians, especially to the Siberians. These tasty morsels imply feasting accompanied by endless shots of vodka.

During the nineteenth century, in Perm, a Siberian city, *pelmeny* were often a part of the pre-wedding celebrations, especially at the feast called the 'bride's farewell.' Zabylin, in his book *Russian People* (1880), writes, 'The young maiden customarily gives a farewell speech to her virginity at her aunt's home in which she addresses all the women present. She is served beer and wine with *pelmeny*.' This tradition no longer exists, although *pelmeny* are still sometimes consumed at wedding feasts and related celebrations.

There is no comparison between homemade handmade (not shaped using a form) *pelmeny* and the packaged *pelmeny* sold in stores and at street kiosks. Some restaurants have managed to create good *pelmeny*, but it's not just the dumplings that make this dish special, it is all the handwork and anticipation that go into the preparation.

Making *pelmeny* at home is no easy chore – the more hands the better. Usually it's a family affair that lasts all day long, and enough *pelmeny* are made and frozen to last about a month. Whenever I start to make these dumplings, my mouth begins to water, and as soon as the first five are made, I've got the perfect excuse to boil them to see how they taste.

One of my Russian friends, Antonina, a native of Perm, makes the best *pelmeny*. Sitting at the table in her cozy kitchen, conversation flowed effortlessly while our fingers never stopped shaping dumplings. While we worked, Antonina reminisced about how she used to make *pelmeny* with her family in Siberia. As they made them, they would throw them out the kitchen window into the snow, to freeze them for later enjoyment.

There are basically two ways of serving *pelmeny* – in a bowl with a broth, or as a plain pasta dish. Either way, *pelmeny* are usually accompanied by a small decanter of white vinegar, hot Russian mustard, copious amounts of sour cream, butter, and freshly ground black pepper. My personal preference is with vinegar, mustard, a small dollop of sour cream, and fresh dill sprinkled on top. Oh, and don't forget the vodka!

Some things to know about making *pelmeny*

■ Double-grinding the filling makes it light and smooth (versus heavy and chunky). If you don't have a meat grinder, place the onions in the bowl of a food processor and pulse until minced. Add the meat and pulse, scraping down the sides of the bowl as needed, until the meat and onions are smooth, light, and fluffy. Add the carbonated water and fresh herbs and pulse a few more times. Cover and refrigerate.

■ Roll the dough out as thin as possible before filling your *pelmeny*. If you don't have time to make dough from scratch, use wonton wrappers and proceed with the instructions below to assemble the *pelmeny*, folding them into triangles instead of half-circles. You will need to brush the edges of the wrappers with water to seal the filling inside the dough.

■ Try to make your *pelmeny* as small as possible, because like all types of pasta, they grow in the pot.

■ Cook a couple of *pelmeny* in boiling water to check the seasoning before you shape them all.

■ *Pelmeny* can be made up to one month in advance and kept frozen until it is time to cook them. They should be served immediately after cooking.

Meat Filling

MAKES ABOUT 95 *PELMENY*

½ pound lean ground beef

½ pound lean ground pork

1 large onion, cut into quarters

1½ teaspoons salt

1 teaspoon freshly ground pepper

½ cup carbonated water

3 tablespoons chopped fresh dill

3 tablespoons chopped fresh parsley

Pasta Dough

2 eggs

½ teaspoon salt

2¼ cups all-purpose flour, plus about ¾ cup for assembling the
pelmeny

Cooking Broth

2 quarts water or stock

2 bay leaves

7 black peppercorns

1 teaspoon salt

For Serving

Chopped fresh dill and parsley, for garnish

Distilled white vinegar

Russian mustard or other hot mustard

Sour cream

Unsalted butter

Freshly ground pepper

To make the meat filling, grind the beef and pork through a
meat grinder, followed by the onion. Combine the meat and

onion in a medium bowl, add the salt, pepper, carbonated water, dill, and parsley, and mix by hand until all the ingredients are very well incorporated and the mixture is smooth. Cover and refrigerate. (The meat filling can be made up to 6 hours in advance.)

To make the pasta dough, put the eggs in a measuring cup and add enough water to make 1 cup. Pour the egg-water mixture into a large bowl and whisk until fluffy. Add the salt and flour and mix with a wooden spoon until the dough begins to come together. Using your hands, knead the dough in the bowl or on a lightly floured work surface until all the flour is well incorporated and the dough is smooth. Form the dough into a ball, and cover it with plastic wrap.

To assemble the *pelmeny*, dust two large trays with flour; set aside. Dust your work surface with flour. Using a sharp long knife, cut the ball of dough into 5 equal portions. Working with one portion at a time (keep the others covered), roll the dough into a 12-inch log, about ¾ inch thick. Coat the blade of a small knife with flour and cut the log into ½-inch-wide slices; you should have about 18 pieces.

Working with one piece at a time, dip the cut sides of the dough in flour, flatten it into a circle, and then, using a rolling pin, roll the dough out to a 3-inch round, as thin as possible. Pick up the dough round, place a heaping ½ teaspoonful of filling in the center, and fold the dough over to form a half-circle.

Seal the edges of the dough by pinching them together. The dough should be moist enough that the edges stick together without having to use any water or egg wash. If not, moisten lightly with water to seal the edges. Place the folded side of the half-circle over your thumb to create an arch, then finish shaping the dumpling by bringing the two corners together in the front and pinching them tightly together. The finished dumpling should resemble the shape of tortellini. Place the filled dumplings on the floured tray. Once each tray is full, set it aside if cooking immediately, or place the tray in the freezer; after the *pelmeny* are completely frozen, transfer them to freezer bags and store them in the freezer for up to one month.

To cook the *pelmeny*, combine the water, bay leaves, peppercorns, and salt in a pot and bring to a boil. Cook the *pelmeny* in batches: add no more than 20 *pelmeny* to the pot at a time and return to a boil, then reduce the heat to medium-high, and cook, uncovered, until all of the dumplings float to the surface, about 3 minutes if fresh, and 5 minutes if frozen. Check for doneness by trying one. Remove with a slotted spoon and place the dumplings in heated serving bowls. Bring the water to a full boil over high heat before adding each new batch.

Pelmeny should be served immediately. Garnish with the fresh herbs and pass the vinegar, mustard, sour cream, butter, and pepper at the table.

What Russians Drink

When God created the world, He made different nations and gave them all sorts of different things – land, corn, and fruit. Then, He asked them if they were satisfied, and they all said yes, except the Russians, who had got just as much as the rest, but replied, 'Please Lord, some vodka.'

– Popular Russian tale

Vodka

N O RUSSIAN FEAST IS COMPLETE WITHOUT VODKA. Russians are notorious for their consumption of vodka, and only two types exist – good, or export quality, and bad. A popular 'good' brand is Pshenichnaya, or wheat vodka, and, of course, there is Stolichnaya. Pshenichnaya comes in half-liter bottles, sometimes with a nonresealable cap, which epitomizes the Russian attitude that a whole bottle must be finished in one sitting. It is not unheard of to see three strangers chip in to buy a bottle of vodka and drink it right there on the pavement in front of the store.

But for most Russians, vodka is enjoyed at the table accompanied by good friends and good food. Russians are eager to educate their foreign guests on the art of downing a shot of vodka, and they believe that practice makes perfect. Following is some advice on how to drink vodka offered by the court stenographer in Anton Chekhov's short story, *The Siren's Song*.

> Well, sir, when you enter the house the table must already be set, and when you sit down, at once tuck the napkin behind your cravat and reach out without hurry for the little decanter with vodka. But don't pour it, the darling, into a little wine glass, but into some sort of antediluvian silver mug heirloom or some pot-bellied little glass with an inscription 'Monks Also Partake of This,' and drink it not at a gulp, but first you sigh, rub your hands, look at the ceiling un-concernedly, then, still without hurrying, raise it, the vodka, that is, to the lips and at once sparks fly from your stomach throughout the whole body.

Beer

Beer is considered a man's drink. Domestically produced beer, called *pivo*, is usually sold at kiosks out of 300-liter drums oper-ated by a foot pump. Customers supply their own container, be it a glass for a quick drink or a jug for a party. Garlands of dried salted fish called *vobla*, the traditional accompaniment to beer, are hung like Christmas lights in some of the kiosk windows.

Eating *vobla* is an art in itself. First, holding the fish by the tail, you have to whack it on a hard surface to free the meat from the bone. Next, you pull off the dorsal fins to open the fish, and then peel off the skin. Finally, you tear out the fillet, best described as a chewy fish jerky, and eat it on the spot. Unless, of course, you want to eat it later. For future enjoyment, some Russians wrap the *vobla* in a piece of newspaper and carry it around in their brief-cases, undeterred by the foul odor. Friends once gave me some *vobla* as a practical joke, but I couldn't keep it in the house even for a minute, because it reeked.

Kvas

Kvass, along with mead and beer, has been drunk since *Kievan Rus'* [period of Russian history dating from the ninth century to the thirteenth century]. Whereas the nobility in earlier times preferred mead, the common people drank *kvass*. It was the most popular drink in nineteenth-century Russia, consumed by the rich as an occasional refreshment and by the peasantry on a daily basis. Like the gathering of mushrooms and berries, the eating of *prjaniki*, and the consumption of *shchi*, the drinking of *kvass* in late Tsarist Russia had become a culture-laden act that helped to define one's Russianness. Although *kvass* was easily made at home, the itinerant *kvass* peddler was a common figure in the streets and markets.

– Classic Russian Cooking, Elena Molokhovets' *A Gift to Young Housewives*, translated and introduced by Joyce Toomre

In the nineteenth century, brewing *kvas*, a lightly fermented drink similar to beer, was considered an art. The objective was to produce colorful bottles of *kvas* flavored with fruits such as berries, raisins, pears, apples, and lemons or with beets, mint, honey, or molasses. Whatever the flavor, the base of most *kvas* brews was black bread or grain, sometimes yeast was added.

Until recently, *kvas* was sold from vending machines, from trucks parked alongside the road, or from kiosks on street corners. Most of these vending machines and *kvas* trucks are broken or have been shut down for unsanitary conditions. Bottled *kvas* is readily available in grocery stores, or Russians can buy a convenient starter package or bottled starter, which is added to water and left to ferment. The results are, at best, nondescript.

Fruit Juice and Herbal Brews

> A lad of seventeen in a handsome pink cotton shirt brought and set down before them a few decanters of soft fruit drinks of all sorts and colors, some as thick as oil and others as fizzy as lemonade. Having set down the decanters, he picked up a spade which was leaning against a tree and went off into the garden
>
> – Nikolay Gogol, *Dead Souls*

Packaged fruit juices and bottled fruit syrups, both imported and domestically produced, are readily available in stores, but many Russians prefer to make their own *sok*, or fruit juice, by adding crushed berries or fruit compote (made from fresh or dried fruits) to water. Usually pieces of whole fruit are left in the drink to be eaten with a spoon from the bottom of the empty glass.

Russians are also fond of herbal brews and exotic flavored waters, such as *beryozovy sok*, or birch water. To make it, a birch branch is cut off the tree and the end is inserted into a small-necked jar (like a Coke bottle). Rain runs down the branch and washes the cut, then rolls off into the jar, perfumed with birch essence. It sounds funky, but it tastes good, woodsy and slightly sweet from the sap.

Many people make their own tisanes and herbal brews. In summer, my friend Natalya often prepares a concoction of St. John's wort *(Hypericum perforatum)*, various leaves (mint, red and black currant, raspberry, and strawberry), rose hips, and lime juice. All or some of these ingredients are added to boiling water and left to steep for a couple of days, then strained and served cold, like iced tea. Sometimes Natalya stirs in a spoonful of black currant *varenye* for color.

Water

For most Russians, bottled noncarbonated water is considered an imported luxury and a waste of money. (Russian carbonated water has a very high salt content, my mother aptly calls it seawater.) While Russian tap water leaves much to be desired, well water from the countryside and blessed water from various city springs are a treat. During the summer months, Russians visiting their *dachas* almost always carry back gallons of well water to the city. They say it is healthier and tastes better than municipal water, and they are right.

Tenants of the high-rise apartment buildings in many of Moscow's suburbs get their summer drinking water from natural streams near their homes. In the Krilatskoye district, about twenty minutes from the city center, Russians can be seen walking to a spring in the nearby hills carrying empty bottles and jugs. Spring boxes, often no more than a circle of large stones that collect the water in a pool, are sometimes protected by a lean-to and an icon, or sometimes an icon or cross is simply nailed to a tree close by. When berries are in season, Russians crush them in the water to perfume it.

Flavored Vodka

Flavoring vodka is a centuries-old tradition in Russia. Pear leaves, tree bark, and spices, such as nutmeg and cloves, were commonly used in the past. Nowadays, the most popular infusions are made with caraway seeds, hot pepper, lemon and orange zest, and fruit, including strawberries, raspberries, cranberries, and cherries. The various colored and flavored vodkas are served from crystal decanters.

Flavored vodkas were and still are believed to have medicinal qualities. Here is how Pulkheria Ivanovna, the lady of the house in Nikolay Gogol's *Old-World Landowners*, tells it:

'This,' she would say, taking a cork out of a bottle, 'is vodka distilled with milfoil [yarrow] and sage – if anyone has a pain in the shoulder blades or loins, it is very good; now this is distilled with centaury – if anyone has a ringing in the ears or a rash on the face, it is very good; and this now is distilled with peach stones – take a glass, isn't it a delicious smell? If anyone getting up in the morning knocks his head against a corner of the cupboard or a table and a bump comes up on his forehead, he has only to drink one glass of it before dinner and it takes it away entirely; it all passes off that very minute, as though it had never been there at all.'

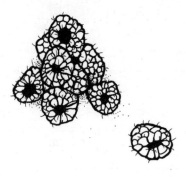

Strawberry Vodka

[KLUBNICHNAYA VODKA]

Making berry-flavored vodka is very easy. A mash of fruit and sugar is added to plain vodka and left to stand for five days. Then the vodka is strained, poured into a decanter, and chilled until ready to serve. Cheaper vodka really benefits from this treatment.

Cooking Note: Standing time 5 days.

MAKES 1 LITER

1½ pounds ripe strawberries, washed and hulled
½ cup sugar
One 1-liter bottle 80- or 90-proof vodka

Place the strawberries and sugar in a food processor or blender and process to a chunky puree, about 1 minute. Transfer the puree to a 1½-quart decanter or jar with a tight-fitting lid. Pour in the vodka, stir, and seal tightly. Let stand at room temperature for 5 days.

After 5 days, strain the vodka. Line a fine-mesh sieve with a double layer of cheesecloth and set it over a bowl. Strain a small portion of the vodka into the bowl, then gently squeeze out the liquid from the cheesecloth. Transfer the strained vodka to a clean decanter or jar with a tight-fitting lid. Discard the strawberry pulp, rinse the cheesecloth with cold water, wring it out tightly, and reline the sieve with the cheesecloth. Strain the remaining vodka repeating these steps.

Seal tightly. Chill before serving.

Variations

Raspberry Vodka: Substitute 12 ounces raspberries for the strawberries. Do not wash the raspberries.

Cranberry Vodka: Substitute one 12-ounce bag cranberries, rinsed, for the strawberries. The berries should be soft and fairly sweet, not hard and bitter. Use 2 cups sugar for the mash.

Cherry Vodka: Substitute 1 pound ripe dark cherries for the strawberries. Wash and stem the cherries, but do not pit them. Mash the cherries with a potato masher or wooden spoon or squeeze them with your fingers to break them up. Add the sugar and stir until completely dissolved. Transfer to a decanter, add the vodka, and proceed as directed.

Orange Vodka

[APELSINNAYA VODKA]

Nothing could be simpler than citrus-flavored vodka. Just be sure to remove only the colored zest of the fruit, leaving the bitter white pith behind.

Cooking Note: Standing time 3 days

MAKES 1 LITER

One 1-liter bottle 80- or 90-proof vodka
Zest of 1 large juice orange, removed with a peeler or zester and cut into ⅛-inch dice
½ cup fresh orange juice
2 tablespoons sugar

Pour the vodka into a 1½-quart decanter or jar with a lid. Add the orange zest, orange juice, and sugar. Seal tightly and shake until the sugar is almost completely dissolved. Let stand at room temperature for 3 days.

Strain the vodka through a fine-mesh sieve. Transfer to a clean bottle or decanter and seal tightly. Chill before serving.

Variations

Lemon Vodka: Substitute the zest of 1 large lemon and ⅓ cup fresh lemon juice for the orange zest and juice. Increase the amount of sugar to ½ cup.

Lime Vodka: Substitute the zest of 1 large lime and ⅓ cup lime juice for the orange zest and juice. Increase the amount of sugar to ½ cup.

Epilogue

Through reason Russia can't be known,
No common yardstick can avail you:
She has a nature all her own –
Have faith in her, all else will fail you.
– Fyodor Tyutchev, 'Russia'

USSIAN FOOD, LIKE ANY UNFAMILIAR CUISINE, is best
enjoyed with an image in mind of how native
Russians savor it. As these vignettes show, Russia's
finest dishes have been preserved and passed down through the
feast days of the Russian Orthodox Church and through
the gentle rhythms of country life. They have been kept alive by
a resilient people who have refused to let hardship, Communism,
or anything else get in the way of their traditions.

Celebrations take on a special poignancy in Russia, where food
is an expression of life. Russians gather around tables to celebrate
life's passages – birthdays and weddings, Easter, and the New Year.
Experience has taught Russians to appreciate the importance of the
small things in life that bring joy – be it a beautiful garden, tall
kulichi, perfect jars of *varenye*, a just-pulled-from-the-garden beet
or potato, or a basketful of wild mushrooms. These small treasures
and social gatherings erase some of the everyday hardships, and
perhaps ease the painful memories of suffering and loss that have

left no Russian unaffected.

On a personal note, Paul Jones, the American friend I accompanied to the vegetarian dinner in a communal apartment and to the *bliny* festival in Suzdal, is now my husband. We were married in 1995 in a traditional Russian Orthodox wedding ceremony at Saint Nicholas Orthodox Cathedral in Washington, D.C. Blessed to have spent three years in the land of my forebears, I left Russia with a renewed sense of my family's traditions and a determination to pass them on to my children, just as my grandmother and mother did for me.

Menus

There is no secret formula for serving the recipes in *A Year of Russian Feasts*. Simply let your taste buds guide you. However, if you want to create authentic Russian feasts, use the following menus as a starting point. Tailor them to make your meals as simple or elaborate as you wish. Recipes for dishes followed by an * can be found in this book. Use your favorite recipes for others. Some of the suggested dishes can be purchased from a grocery or specialty food store, preferably one that has a Russian or Eastern European foods section.

Zakuski **Suggestions:** To begin a Russian dinner, a spread of small dishes is usually laid out on the table before guests sit down. This first-course assortment traditionally includes: whole, small, lightly salted cucumbers or deli-style cucumbers, salted tomatoes, salted cabbage (not sauerkraut), cabbage salads, salted mushrooms or marinated mushrooms, smoked fish (trout, salmon, or sturgeon), herring in sour cream, red or black caviar (preferably ossetra), deli-style cold cuts (such as ham or salami), cheese (*sulguni* or Bulgarian feta), and a fresh vegetable platter. Composed and other salads can also be part of the *zakuski* course placed on the table.

Main-Course Suggestions: Grilled or broiled meat (beef, lamb, or pork), poultry, and fish are commonly served as main courses. Main-course recipes in this book include: Chicken with Walnuts, Garlic, and Fresh Cilantro, Meat-Filled Dumplings from Siberia, and Masha's Vegetable Ragout.

Dessert Suggestions: Dessert usually consists of fresh fruit (when in season), or store-bought cakes, cookies, or chocolates. Russian Cream with Summer Berries, Walnut Cake, and Snow Cookies are some traditional Russian desserts included in this book. Tea is usually offered with dessert.

Beverage Suggestions: Russian vodka (plain or flavoured) is always served at a feast. Wine (white or red) and sparkling wine are often offered. Popular Russian soft drinks include *kvas* (a slightly fermented non-alcoholic drink), *mors* (a berry or fruit drink), and American soda pop. Water (usually bottled mineral water) is not automatically placed on the table, but rather served if requested. To Russians, more important than the beverage is the round of toasting that accompanies it. If you are hosting a party, be sure to have some toasts in mind, and some pickles or other salty foods – which are usually part of the *zakuski* – to be eaten as a chaser (see The Art of Russian Toasting, page 00).

Russian Tea Suggestions: A tea party Russian-style can be as simple or elaborate as desired, incorporating sweet and savory delicacies. *Varenye*, or Russian fruit preserves, are served in small bowls at each individual place setting. See pages 96-97 for instructions on how to brew tea Russian-style.

Typical Russian Menus

Russian Breakfast
Choice of pancakes:
   Everyday Pancakes with a Sweet Cheese Filling*
   Butter Week Pancakes*
   Silver Dollar Pancakes*
   Cheese Pancakes with Blueberry Sauce*
Choice of baked goods:
   Russian Name Day Bread*
   A Walnut Birthday Cake*
   Russian-Style Apple Pie*
Strawberry or Apricot Jam*
Platter of cold cuts and cheese
Red caviar or smoked fish (salmon or sturgeon)
Eggs any style
Fresh fruit
Bread basket
Coffee or Russian-Style Tea*

Russian Lunch
Choice of soup:
   Russian Cabbage Soup*
   Mushroom Soup*
   My Grandmother's Beet Soup*
Little Meat-Filled Russian Pies* or any hearty bread
Smoked salmon or sturgeon on buttered black bread garnished
   with fresh dill
Platter of cold cuts and cheese
Russian-Style Chicken Salad*
Green salad with a light vinaigrette
Fresh fruit

Russian Dinner I

Assortment of *zakuski* (see *Zakuski* Suggestions above). Include choice(s) of:

    Beet Salad with Walnuts and Garlic*

    Russian-Style Chicken Salad*

Russian Cabbage Soup*

Grilled or broiled filet mignon, lamb chops, chicken, or fish

Potatoes Russian-Style*

Individual Mushroom Casseroles*

Russian Cream with Summer Berries*

Russian Dinner II

Assortment of *zakuski* (see *Zakuski* Suggestions above). Include choice(s) of:

    Carrot, Beet, and Potato Salad*

    Two Russian-Style Cabbage Salads*

    Marinated Mushrooms*

My Grandmother's Beet Soup*

Chicken with Walnuts, Garlic, and Fresh Cilantro*

Bread (such as *lavash*), *kasha**, or rice

Russian Cream with Summer Berries*

Vegetarian Dinner

Assortment of *zakuski* (see *Zakuski* Suggestions above). Include choice(s) of:

    Eggplant Caviar*

    Carrot, Beet, and Potato Salad*

    Two Russian-Style Cabbage Salads*

    Vegetable *Zakuski**

Masha's Vegetable Ragout*

Kasha*, rice, or pasta

Green salad with a light vinaigrette

Russian Cream with Summer Berries* or fresh fruit

Christmas Dinner

Assortment of *zakuski* (see *Zakuski* Suggestions above). Include choice(s) of:

    Beet Salad with Walnuts and Garlic*

    Eggplant Caviar*

Mushroom Soup*

Meat-Filled Dumplings from Siberia*

Christmas Porridge*

Snow Cookies*

Easter Feast

Assortment of *zakuski* (see *Zakuski* Suggestions above). Include choice(s) of:

    Butter Week Pancakes* with black or red caviar

    Carrot, Beet, and Potato Salad*

Main course possibilities

    Grilled or broiled lamb chops or roasted leg of lamb with Potato Casserole with Mushroom Sauce*

    Chicken with Walnuts, Garlic, and Fresh Cilantro* with Bread (*lavash*), *kasha**, or rice

Russian Easter Bread* or store-bought *panettone* (Italian Christmas bread)

    Russian Easter Cheesecake*

Russian-Style Apple Pie*

Russian Tea

Cheese Pancakes with Blueberry Sauce*

Choice of baked goods (or substitute store-bought):

    Russian Name Day Bread*

    A Walnut Birthday Cake*

    Russian-Style Apple Pie*

    Cabbage Pie*

The Art of Brewing Tea*

Choice of fruit preserves (or substitute store-bought):
  Strawberry Preserves*
  Apricot Preserves*
Snow Cookies* or store-bought cookies

Approximate Metric Equivalents

Metrics have been rounded to the nearest decimal point for most of these conversions.

LIQUID INGREDIENTS		DRY INGREDIENTS	
U.S.	METRIC	U.S.	METRIC
U.S. MEASUREMENT	MILLILITERS/LITERS	OUNCES	GRAMS
¼ teaspoon	1.0 ml.	¼ oz.	7 g.
½ teaspoon	2.5	½	14
¾ teaspoon	4.0	¾	21
1 teaspoon	5.0	1	28
1¼ teaspoons	6.0	1½	43
1½ teaspoons	7.5	2	57
1¾ teaspoons	8.5	3	85
2 teaspoons	10.0	4	113
1 tablespoon	15.0	5	142
2 tablespoons	30.0	6	170
¼ cup (2 ounces)	59.0	7	198
⅓ cup	79.0	8	227
½ cup (4 ounces)	118.0	9	255
⅔ cup	158.0	10	284
¾ cup (6 ounces)	178.0	11	312
1 cup (8 ounces)	237.0	12	340
1½ cups	355.0	13	369
2 cups (1 pint)	473.0	14	397
3 cups	710.0	15	425
4 cups (1 quart)	0.95 l.	16 (1 lb.)	454
1.06 quarts	1.0 l.		
4 quarts (1 gallon)	3.8 l.		

POUNDS	KILOGRAMS
1 lb.	0.45 kg.
2	0.91
3	1.4
4	1.8
5	2.3

Note 2.2 pounds equals 1 kilogram

Oven Temperatures

OVEN HEAT	FAHRENHEIT	CELSIUS	GAS MARK
Warming Foods	200° to 250°	93° to 121°	0 to ¼
Very Low	250° to 275°	121° to 133°	½ to 1
Warm	300° to 325°	149° to 163°	2 to 3
Moderate	350° to 375°	177° to 190°	4 to 5
Hot	400° to 425°	204° to 218°	6 to 7
Very Hot	450° to 475°	232° to 246°	8 to 9
Extremely Hot	500° to 525°	260° to 274°	10

FAHRENHEIT/CELSIUS CONVERSION FORMULAS

Celsius to Fahrenheit: add 32 and multiply by 1.8
Fahrenheit to Celsius: subtract 32 and multiply by 0.5556

Bibliography

Library of Foreign Literature, Moscow

Baring, Maurice. **The Russian People.** Methuen and Co., Ltd., London, 1911.

Barry, Herbert. **Russia in 1870.** Wyman and Sons, London, 1871.

Bouton, John Bell. **Roundabout to Moscow, an Epicurean Journey.** D. Appleton and Company, New York, 1887.

Clowes, William, and Murray, John. **A Memoir of the Life of Peter the Great, The Family Library No. XXXV, Peter the Great.** London, MDCCCXXXII.

Coxe, William. **Travels into Poland, Russia, and Sweden and Denmark,** illustrated with charts and engravings. 5 vols. 1792.

Dowager Marchioness of Dufferin and Ava. **My Russian and Turkish Journals.** John Murray, London, 1916.

Frankland, Captain C. Colville, R.N. **Narrative of a Visit to the Courts of Russia and Sweden in the Years 1830 and 1831.** Henry Colburn and Richard Bently, London, 1832.

Heard, James Arthur, Knight of the Order of Saint Stanislaus. **The Life and Times of Nathalie Borissovna, Princess Dolgorookov.** Bosworth and Harrison, London, 1857.

Kennard, Howard P., M.D. **The Russian Peasant.** T. Werner Laurie, London, 1907.

Lansbury, Violet. **An Englishwoman in the USSR.** Putnam, London, 1940.

Mackenzie, Donald Wallace. **Russia, Vol. I and Vol. II.** Cassell, Petter, and Galpin, London, 1877.

Murray, John. **Journal of a Tour in Germany, Sweden, Russia, and Poland During the Years 1813 and 1814.** J.T. James, Esq.,

Student of Christ Church Oxford in Two Volumes. 2d ed. London, 1817.

Raikes, Thomas, Esq. **A Visit to Saint Petersburg in the Winter of 1829 and 1830.** Richard Bentley, 'Publisher in Ordinary to Her Majesty,' London, 1838.

Richard, John. **A Tour from London to Petersburg, from Thence to Moscow and Return to London by Way of Poland, Germany, and Holland.** 1778.

Stepniak. **The Russian Peasantry, Their Agrarian Condition, Social Life, and Religion.** Swan Sonnenschein and Co., London, 1888.

Sitwell, Sacheverell. **Valse des Fleurs, a Day in Saint Petersburg and a Ball at the Winter Palace in 1868.** Faber and Faber Ltd., London, 1941.

Wilmont, Catherine and Martha. **The Russian Journals of Martha and Catherine Wilmont 1803–1808.** Macmillan and Co., Ltd., London, 1935.

The Englishwoman in Russia, Impressions of the Society and Manners of the Russians at Home by a Lady 10 Years Resident in that Country. John Murray, London, 1855.

Russia as Seen and Described by Famous Writers, edited and translated by Esther Singleton. New York, Dodd Mead and Co., 1909.

Russian Literature

Chekhov, Anton. **The Party and Other Stories.** Translated by Ronald Wilks. London: Penguin Books, 1985.

———. **Anton Chekhov's Short Stories.** Selected and edited by Ralph E. Matlaw. New York: W.W. Norton & Company, Inc., 1979.

———. **Anton Chekhov Collected Works in Five Volumes,**

Volume Four, Stories 1895-1903. Translated by Olga Shartse and Ivy Litvinov. Moscow: Raduga Publishers, 1979.

Dostoyevsky, Fyodor. **Poor Folk and Other Stories.** Translated by David McDuff. London: Penguin Books, 1988.

Gogol, Nikolay. **Christmas Eve, Stories from Village Evenings Near Dikanka and Mirgorod.** Translated by Christopher English and Angus Roxburgh. Moscow: Raduga Publishers, 1991.

———. **The Complete Tales of Nikolai Gogol, Volume 2.** The Constance Garnett translation has been revised throughout by the editor, Leonard J. Kent. Chicago: University of Chicago Press, 1985.

———. **Dead Souls.** Translated by David Magarshack. London: Penguin Books, 1961.

Lermontov, Mikhail. **Three Russian Poets, Selections from Pushkin, Lermontov and Tyutchev.** Translated by Vladimir Nabokov. New York: New Directions, 1944.

Nabokov, Vladimir. **Speak, Memory.** New York: Vintage International, 1989.

Pushkin, Aleksander. **Eugene Onegin, A Novel in Verse.** Translated by Vladimir Nabokov. Princeton, N.J.: Princeton/Bollingen Paperback Edition, 1990.

Tolstoy, Aleksey Nikolayevich. **Nikita's Childhood.** Translated by M. Skobelev and A. Yeliseyev. Moscow: Foreign Languages Publishing House.

Tolstoy, Aleksey Konstantinovich. **Aleksey Konstantinovich Tolstoy, Complete Set of Verses in Two Volumes.** Leningrad: Soviet Writers, 1984.

The Oxford Dictionary of Phrase, Saying, and Quotation. Edited by Elizabeth Knowles. Oxford: Oxford University Press, 1997.

Other Sources

Blanksteen, Jane. **Nothing Beets Borscht.** Atheneum, New York, 1974.

Chamberlain, Leslie. **The Food and Cooking of Russia.** Crown Publishers, New York, 1979.

Dubois, Urbain. **La Cuisine Classique.** E. Dentu, Paris, 1874.

Fisher, M. F. K. **The Art of Eating, An Alphabet for Gourmets,** Vintage Books, New York, 1976.

Gagarina, Mariia, Princess Alexandra. **The Borzoi Cookbook.** Heinemann, Ltd., London, 1924.

Goldstein, Darra. **A Taste of Russia: A Cookbook of Russian Hospitality.** Harper Perennial, New York, 1991.

Gould-Marks, Beryl. **Eating the Russian Way.** Roy Publishers, New York, 1964/65.

Lapenkova, Valentina. **Russian Food and Drink.** Bookwright Press, New York, 1988.

Lobanov-Rostovskii, Alexandr. **Tablettes Gastronomique de Saint-Petersburg.** Rare Book Collection.

Massie, Suzanne. **Land of the Firebird: The Beauty of Old Russia.** Simon and Schuster, New York, 1982.

Nicolaieff, Nina. **Art of Russian Cooking.** Doubleday, New York, 1969.

Papashvily, Helen. **Russian Cooking.** Time-Life Books, Inc., New York, 1969.

Petit, Alphonse. **La Gastronomie en Russie.** L'Arche du Livre, Paris, 1970.

Petrovna, Nina. **Russian Cookery.** Penguin Books, Baltimore, 1968.

Selivanova, Nina. **Dining and Wining in Old Russia.** E.P. Dutton and Co., 1933

Skipwith, Sofka. **Eat Russian.** Newton Abbot, England, 1973.

Toomre, Joyce. **Classic Russian Cooking, Elena Molokhovet's A**

Gift to Young Housewives. Indiana University Press, Indianapolis, 1992.

Troyat, Henry. **Daily Life in Russia under the Last Tsar.** Stanford University Press, Stanford, California, 1979.

Uvezain, Sonia. **The Best Foods of Russia.** Harcourt, Brace, and Janovich, New York, 1976.

Volokh, Anne. **The Art of Russian Cooking.** Macmillan, New York, 1983.

Zabylin, M. **Russky Narod. Ego obychai, obryady, predaniya, suyeveriya i poeziya (The Russian People. Its customs, ceremonies, traditions, superstitions, and poetry).** Izdaniye knigoprodavtsa M. Berezina, Moscow, 1880.

Russian Samovar. Sovetskaya Rossiya, Moscow, 1991.

About the Author

Some of my first memories of cooking date to times spent with my grandmother in Antigua as she cooked Russian food for my grandfather, Nikita Cheremeteff. Nikita was a trim, handsome man who enjoyed life to its fullest. The great-great grandson of Czar Nicholas I, Nikita was born in St. Petersburg and spent his childhood there. Just prior to the 1917 Revolution, his parents anticipated the upheaval and sent their only son to attend the Naval Academy in Finland.

After graduating, Nikita and an archeologist friend sailed around the Aegean Sea investigating ancient sites. While in Greece, Nikita met a stunning brunette, Katherine Vandoro, whose family had fled Yalta to escape Stalin's persecutions. Nikita and Katherine were married in Athens and had four children: Marie (my mother), Vladimir, Alexandra, and Sergei. The Cheremeteff family relocated to London until 1964, when Nikita, a marine engineer on a mission in the Caribbean Sea, discovered the island of Antigua and retired there. Katherine and her youngest son, Sergei, still reside on Antigua.

After graduating from Connecticut College, I began my food career in 1987 in Paris, where I attended La Varenne cooking school. Upon returning to the United States, I worked for the late Jean-Louis Palladin at Jean-Louis at the Watergate in Washington, D.C. I first worked in his kitchen and then designed and tested the recipes for *Jean-Louis: Cooking with the Seasons* (Thomasson Grant, Charlottesville, Virginia, 1989).

Born in New Delhi, I became accustomed to a life of constant travel from a tender age. My father, retired Ambassador Brandon Grove, Jr., was stationed in the Ivory Coast, India, East and West Berlin, Jerusalem, and Zaire. Today, I travel the world with my husband, Paul Jones, a foreign service officer, and our two children, Aleksandra and Hale. Our last overseas assignment was in Skopje, Macedonia.

$Index$

BITTER ALMONDS
RECOLLECTIONS AND RECIPES
FROM A SICILIAN GIRLHOOD
by Mary Taylor Simeti and Maria Grammatico

Bitter Almonds is the true story of a woman's extraordinary courage, and a gift from the past of an almost-lost tradition. At the heart of the book are 50 recipes of unique Sicilian specialities, written down for the first time.

In the early 1950s, Maria Grammatico and her sister were sent by their impoverished mother to the San Carlo, a cloistered orphanage in Erice, an ancient hill town on the western coast of Sicily. It was a Dickensian existence – beating sugar mixtures for six hours at a time, rising before dawn to prime the ovens, and surviving on an unrelenting diet of vegetable gruel. But it was here that Maria learned to make the beautifully handcrafted pastries that were sold to customers from behind a grille in the convent wall.

At 22, Maria left the orphanage with no personal possessions, minimal schooling and no skills other than what she carried in her head and hands – the knowledge acquired during a childhood spent preparing delicacies for other people's celebrations.

Today, she is the successful owner of her own *pasticceria* in Erice, a mecca for travellers the world over. Her counters are piled high with home-made *biscotti*, tarts, cakes, and jams – Torta Divina, Cassata Siciliana, Cotognata. A frequent customer, Mary Taylor Simeti became first friend and then chronicler of Maria's moving story.

Bitter Almonds is a remarkable memoir, a tribute to Sicilian food and culture, and the record of an historic and vanishing craft.

'The poignant story of a Sicilian woman . . . an astonishing account' *New York Times*

A Bantam Paperback

0 553 81465 6

FROM HERE, YOU CAN'T SEE PARIS
By Michael S. Sanders

A fascinating memoir about life in Les Arques (population 159), a hilltop village in a remote corner of France untouched by the modern era. It is the story of a dying community's struggle to survive, of an artist whose legacy begins its rebirth, and of chef Jacques Ratier and his wife, Noelle, whose magical restaurant – the village's sole business – has helped ensure its future.

The author set out to explore the inner workings of a French restaurant kitchen but ended up stumbling into a wider, much richer world. Whether uncovering the darker secrets of *foie gras* or absorbing the lore of the land around a farmhouse kitchen table after a boar hunt, Michael Sanders learned that life in Les Arques was anything but sleepy. You will discover its vibrant history and traditions of food, cooking and rural living, sharing a family's adventures as they find their way in a place that is sometimes lonely, often wondrous, and always fascinating.

'A rich textural tapestry of everyday life in the Lot . . . Honest, funny and endearing'   Ken Hom

A Bantam Paperback

0 553 81566 0

BELLA TUSCANY
By Frances Mayes

Continuing Frances Mayes's account of her love affair with
Italy, *Bella Tuscany* presents the author now truly at home there,
meeting the challenges of learning a new language and touring
regions outside Tuscany, including castle towns, fishing villages
and islands. With fresh adventures and updates on the characters
introduced in *Under the Tuscan Sun*, she also explores new
themes in this wondrous corner of the world, delving into
gardening, wine-making, and the experience of primavera – a
season of renewed possibility. And Frances Mayes reveals more
simple pleasures from her Tuscan kitchen in a section devoted to
recipes. In the sensuous, vivid prose that has become her
hallmark, *Bella Tuscany* celebrates the author's deepening
connection to the land and her flourishing friendships in a new-
found haven of idyllic living.

'There is much to enjoy in this volume, which is part guidebook,
part gardening manual, part cookery book, part history, part
language course, and which rolls along with sustained vigour and
joyous enthusiasm'   *Daily Mail*

'Meanders anecdotally and thoughtfully through a sabbatical
spring and long summer . . . Part travelogue and part intelligent
reflection on the essential quality of Italy and Italians'
Independent

A Bantam Paperback

0 553 81250 5

FRENCH SPIRITS
A House, a Village, and a Love Affair in Burgundy
By Jeffrey Greene

When Jeffrey Greene, a prizewinning American poet, and Mary, his wife-to-be, discover a moss-covered stone presbytery in a lovely village in the Puisaye region of Burgundy, they know they have to live there. With an unabashed *joie de vivre*, they begin the arduous process of procuring their slice of paradise amid the wild beauty of the French countryside.

French Spirits is the magical tale of their odyssey to become not just homeowners but Burgundians, In lyrical prose, Greene recalls their experiences in turning the 300-year-old stone building – which the locals believe houses numerous spirits – into a habitable refuge. He brings to life their adventures in finding wonderful bargains with which to furnish their new space, including a firm mattress and some rather suspicious 'antiques' bought from the back of a van.

Greene offers the unexpected joys and surprises of village life, from celebrating his and Mary's simple backyard wedding to toiling in a verdant garden. He shares the experience of surviving his mother's decision to move in and humorously introduces the locals – both human and non-human – who define his and Mary's new world. Woven throughout this luscious tale are the pleasures of rural France: wondrous food and wine, long-held rituals and feasts, dark superstitions and deeply rooted history. A memorable feast for the senses, *French Spirits* will entertain and enlighten all who succumb to its charms.

'Charming and hilarious'   Michael Korda

A Bantam Paperback

0 553 81479 6

A SELECTED LIST OF NON-FICTION TITLES
AVAILABLE FROM TRANSWORLD

81341 2	LIFE IN A POSTCARD	*Rosemary Bailey*	£7.99
04942 X	AL DENTE	*William Black*	£12.99
40406 7	FIT FOR LIFE COOKBOOK	*Marilyn Diamond*	£8.99
81479 6	FRENCH SPIRITS	*Jeffrey Greene*	£6.99
60476 9	THE FRENCH KITCHEN: A COOK BOOK	*Joanne Harris*	£20.00
81490 7	BEST FOOT FORWARD	*Susie Kelly*	£6.99
04268 9	THE CLAIRE MACDONALD COOKBOOK	*Claire Macdonald*	£25.00
04752 4	SIMPLY SEASONAL	*Claire Macdonald*	£20.00
05022 3	ENTERTAINING SOLO	*Claire Macdonald*	£20.00
99804 4	SEASONAL COOKING	*Claire Macdonald*	£7.99
99217 8	SWEET THINGS	*Claire Macdonald*	£7.99
14428 2	LUNCHES	*Claire Macdonald*	£6.99
14209 3	SUPPERS	*Claire Macdonald*	£7.99
50667 6	UNDER THE TUSCAN SUN	*Frances Mayes*	£6.99
81250 5	BELLA TUSCANY	*Frances Mayes*	£6.99
81448 6	TAKE ME WITH YOU	*Brad Newsham*	£6.99
81417 6	THE GREAT WHITE PALACE	*Tony Porter*	£7.99
04954 3	SWEETS	*Tim Richardson*	£15.00
81550 4	FOUR CORNERS	*Kira Salak*	£6.99
81566 0	FROM HERE, YOU CAN'T SEE PARIS	*Michael Sanders*	£7.99
81356 0	ON PERSEPHONE'S ISLAND	*Mary Taylor Simeti*	£7.99
81465 6	BITTER ALMONDS	*Mary Taylor Simeti & Maria Grammatico*	£6.99
81584 9	WITHOUT RESERVATIONS:	*Alice Steinbach*	£7.99
	THE TRAVELS OF AN INDEPENDENT WOMAN		
81425 7	A COUNTRY LIFE	*Roy Strong*	£6.99
81532 6	CUBA DIARIES	*Isadora Tattlin*	£6.99
50545 9	RED CHINA BLUES	*Jan Wong*	£7.99
40397 4	THE FRAGRANT PHARMACY	*Valerie Ann Worwood*	£9.99
81439 7	LEARNING TO FLOAT	*Lili Wright*	£6.99
81306 4	A LEAF IN THE BITTER WIND	*Ting-Xing Ye*	£8.99